THE ULTIMATE GUIDE TO
REALITY-BASED SELF-DEFENSE

THE ULTIMATE GUIDE TO
REALITY-BASED SELF-DEFENSE

by the Editors of *Black Belt*

Black Belt Books, Valencia CA 91355
Copyright © 2010 Cruz Bay Publishing, Inc
First Printing 2010
All Rights Reserved
Printed in South Korea

Library of Congress Number: 2010938183
ISBN-10: 0-89750-196-9
ISBN-13: 978-0-89750-196-5

Edited by Sarah Dzida, Atina Hartunian and Jeannine Santiago
Cover design by Mher Vahakn
Graphic design by John Bodine

For information about permission to reproduce selections from this book, write Black Belt Books, 24900 Anza Dr. Unit E Valencia, CA. 91355
For information about bulk/wholesale purchases, please contact (800) 423-2874 ext. 1633

BLACK BELT BOOKS
A Division of **OHARA** PUBLICATIONS, INC.
World Leader in Martial Arts Publications

TABLE OF CONTENTS

INTRODUCTION

by the Editors of *Black Belt*

REALITY-BASED TRAINING holds that self-defense is as unpredictable as a tornado and, therefore, predetermined responses to specific attacks may not always be the way to go. That's why it teaches the value of unleashing a relentless offense as soon as danger is detected as well as the differences between engaging in a match fight (both parties agree to get physical) and a street fight (one party attacks the other, often without warning).

At the same time, reality-based self-defense is a broad term, which covers a wide range of topics and tactics from analyzing potentially dangerous situations to learning techniques that achieve optimal strategic self-defense. There are many martial arts—*jeet kune do*, *haganah*, combatives, etc.—that can be classified as reality-based, but no matter what, many of them share the same philosophies. The following list from a 2002 *Black Belt* article by Scott Sonnon outlines the essentials:

1. In any physical conflict, your goal is unconditional survival. It is not to kill an assailant, nor to maim, injure or hurt him, for those are merely byproducts of pursuing your objective.

2. If you do not need to employ your survival tools or if you need to temporarily refrain from using them, they should remain invisible. Only if you are attacked should you allow others to be aware of your ability.

3. By themselves, prearranged self-defense techniques are not sufficient for combat. Unconditional survival demands extensive skill and preparation ranging from nonverbal communication to lethal force.

4. "Symmetrical training" cannot be relied on. Too many martial arts instructors teach you how to use your skills only against practitioners of the same style.

5. Training should not involve any preconceived ideas about saving face or fighting fair. Survival is not about style but about reality.

6. The key to survival does not lie in memorizing a couple quotes from Eastern philosophy, slapping a few flashy kicks and submission holds together, and starting a new style.

7. You must be prepared, psychologically and physiologically, for the attack. Your awareness must be such that you have the ability to function under the intense strain of personal combat even though it will enable you to defuse or avoid 90 percent of all volatile situations.

8. If you understand only fighting skill, then when conflict arises you will fight, even if the situation could have been solved by other means.

9. If you fail to recognize the attack developing and are startled by it, you will not have access to your skills. If you allow your awareness to lapse and fade, you will become a victim of your own overconfidence.

10. Don't spend all your training time in the *dojo*. Miyamoto Musashi, one of humanity's greatest warrior-philosophers, stated in *The Book of Five Rings*: "If you learn indoor techniques, you will think narrowly and forget the true way. Thus you will have difficulty in actual encounters."

11. Martial sports are about technical skill, steadfastness, endurance, doggedness, durability and resilience. They have nothing to do with personal combat because they do not take place outdoors, in the dirt, in the rain, in the snow, on the concrete or in ambush simulations—what Tony Blauer refers to as "ballistic micro-fights."

12. Most people have never fallen on anything harder than a mat. They have never kicked with their shoes on or punched a real person. They have probably not tried to battle from inside a vehicle, from within a crowd of civilians or in the company of untrained loved ones. Don't fall victim to those pitfalls.

13. To prepare for an event, you must simulate it as closely as possible. Performance is in direct proportion to preparation. Moreover, the worst performance you have in training is the best you can hope for in combat.

14. To increase your chance of survival, you must engage in overload practice. Your training simulations must be more difficult than the potential assault.

15. Merely because something is old does not mean it is valuable today. Ancient training methods are an excellent way of learning how people fought and trained in ancient times. Back then, people trained in unarmed fighting because oppressive rulers restricted weapons possession.

16. Some ancient fighting methods are no longer effective because the 21st century has brought a new kind of threat. The assailant who confronts you is "a new breed of felon, more terrorist than criminal," ("Crime in America: It's Going to Get Worse." *Reader's Digest*, August 1995, John DiIulio).

17. Because of the weapons and methods used by modern criminals, you can no longer permit yourself the luxury of training only with your empty hands. You must adopt an integrated system that spans the spectrum of defensive preparation, from nonverbal communication to interpersonal skill to less-than-lethal measures to lethal force.

18. You must always hold true to your goal: to survive unconditionally, without question, at any cost. That does not include fighting; it does include appropriate application of fighting skill at the decisive moment.

19. It's time to fight when the situation is no longer acceptable to you. Rarely do you have to fight. Rarely do you encounter a situation that is truly unacceptable. The obstacle is not that you fail to choose to fight, for it is not a choice but a fact that when something is unacceptable to you, you will act on it in some form.

20. The danger is that when you are surprised or not properly prepared with a flexible and comprehensive combatives doctrine, you are not given the opportunity to "enter the fight." If so, your actions may be inappropriate or insufficient. Anyone can successfully negotiate personal combat—as long as the person is given the ability to act appropriately.

21. What gives you the ability to survive is training within a doctrine that permits you to identify and assess a threat before the fight, one that derails psychological and physiological factors that inhibit your entrance into the fight, one that affords you access to your fighting skill should physical violence break out, and one that provides post-combat knowledge to address legal, medical and social concerns.

22. Your capacity for calmly recognizing an assailant's "probing" process will determine your ability to survive. There are certain characteristics that are common to all attacks and certain brands of behavior common to particular types of belligerents. The attacker's probing phase is one of these characteristics.

23. If the probe returns a positive response, the assailant will select you as his target. If you do not possess the calm repose and wherewithal to recognize that combat begins long before the fight, you will never have access to your fighting skill. If you fail to recognize the development of the attack, you may be able to muster the ability to do something about fighting, but effective retaliation will be beyond the scope of your faculties.

24. Self-protection is not about fighting; it is about awareness and commitment. Awareness of your options and the composition of confrontation increases your survivability. Nonverbal training, eye and facial calibration, body carriage, postural and spatial constitution, gesticulation and verbal skill should be critical parts of your training.

25. Your preparation must encompass the full spectrum of conflict resolution. That can mean feigning submission and acquiescing to the demands of the assailant. Give up your wallet or purse; its contents do not equal your life or the life of a loved one.

26. Withdraw when you can. It may be your most successful tactic. Remember that withdrawal will save your life. In a fight, you will be lucky to leave unscathed, so if you can avoid the fight, do so at all costs. Combat avoided is a fight won.

27. During a physical confrontation that has obvious legal implications, the fight is over when the assailant is no longer a threat, even though the turmoil continues until the situation is resolved legally, socially, physically and emotionally.

28. You should endeavor to end physical confrontation as quickly as possible. Keep your response simple and expedient. You do not have the luxury of being complex, especially in multiple-assailant engagements. Most of the time, you can end the problem by simply unbalancing your adversary and withdrawing tactically.

29. The law never supercedes your right to self-preservation. The legal system was created to perpetuate your survival, not inhibit or endanger it.

30. Fighting is something you do with someone; combat is something you do to someone. Accept no less than unconditional survival. You must if you want to live.

—◦◦◦—

This is why *Black Belt* has selected and complied articles that touch on the fundamental aspects of reality-based self-defense for *The Ultimate Guide to Reality-Based Self-Defense*. As such, the book isn't so much about what specific drills you should memorize in order to come out of a street confrontation alive. Instead, the book will demonstrate how to effectively read dangerous situations, how to avoid them safely, and, in the event that you find yourself in a potentially violent encounter, how to use specific and proven strategies and techniques to come out of it alive.

10 COMMANDMENTS OF REALITY-BASED FIGHTING:
Step-by-Step Instructions for Transforming Yourself Into a Skilled Street Fighter
Part 1

by Richard Ryan • Black Belt September 2008

HOW DO YOU GO from knowing nothing about the martial arts to knowing how to fight? Which path will lead you to the destination in the shortest time? Answering those questions is no easy task, but the 30 years I've spent teaching my self-defense system, Dynamic Combat, have given me some insights that can be helpful.

Before I begin, however, I must explain what "reality-based fighting ," the name I use for this pursuit, means. For years, I've said that the modern martial arts have evolved into three distinct forms: sport fighting (mixed martial arts, or MMA), theatrical martial arts (Xtreme Martial Arts, or XMA—which is what we see in movies and in most modern *kata* competitions) and reality-based fighting (RBF, which refers to systems designed for combat and self-protection). And although each form may have aspects of the others, they're fundamentally different in practice and application.

DEFINING RBF

Reality-based fighting is not sport fighting. I'm not saying that MMA is ineffective, for it obviously is. The vast majority of MMA fighters are highly skilled and have incredible work ethics. The basic skill sets you learn in MMA are great and can transfer to the real world to a certain degree. Problem is, reality fighting often encompasses more than striking and grappling.

Example: In the real world, the location of a fight can hinder the application of many MMA tactics. For confirmation, watch an MMA bout and imagine what would happen if the athletes were on pavement or concrete. What if there were cars nearby? What if the cage was replaced by a brick wall with windows? Note how many times the average MMA match involves one fighter slamming the other to the mat, then think how easy it would be for one of them to shatter a kneecap, fracture a skull or break an elbow if they were battling on the street.

Environment is just one way reality fighting differs from sport fighting. To see the whole picture, remember the four R's: rules, referees, rings and rounds. If any of them is present, what you're doing isn't reality fighting. Competition isn't combat. Sport isn't self-defense. Winning in self-defense means you get to walk away. It means you and perhaps someone you're protecting can go home, hopefully without a severe injury. In the end, it's about surviving.

RBF teaches you about real violence—not the type of violence that happens in a ring or in a movie but the kind that involves real people in the real world. RBF teaches everything that MMA does and everything that it does not. It prepares you for the sucker punch and the fight in which the odds are stacked against you. It teaches you how to deal with weapons, multiple opponents and deception. It teaches you how to manage fear. It acknowledges that people and situations are fundamentally unpredictable. It is practical and pragmatic. It favors ability over athletics, function over form.

Presented below are the first five skill sets you'll need to become an RBF practitioner. They apply as much to the person with no prior martial arts training as they do to those who practice MMA or XMA.

1) LEARN THE LEGAL AND MORAL ISSUES REGARDING USE OF FORCE

Unless you understand the legal and moral aspects of using physical force against another person, you could find yourself in trouble with the law. This is one area in which MMA falls short: Many of the traditional martial arts values such as respect, restraint and humility are nowhere to be found. In or out of the cage, fighting is all that matters.

From a purely combative standpoint, people who study MMA become physically dangerous in a relatively short time. But to borrow a quote from *Spider-Man,* "with great power comes great responsibility." The more skilled you become, the more you should exercise restraint and humility. You need to know what you can and cannot do when it comes to the use of force.

Where can you learn this? The easy answer is to do your homework. In this field, self-education can be effective. Use the Internet to research the laws of your state as they relate to protecting yourself, your family and your property. If you don't understand something, find someone who does—lawyers and police officers are a good bet.

2) LEARN HOW TO STRIKE

In a seminar, karate legend Joe Lewis was once asked whether striking or grappling is more important. He replied, "It's true that a lot of fights end up on the ground, but I guarantee that all of them start standing up."

The acquisition of striking skills should be one of your highest priorities because, short of using a weapon, your hands are the quickest way to end an assault. Most martial arts include striking, but their methods may not be suitable for RBF.

STRIKES: The basic techniques of reality-based fighting often resemble those of sport fighting because stance and positioning are similar. To illustrate, Richard Ryan (left) and Tony Cortina square off once the fight is imminent (1). Cortina steps forward and throws a rear cross, and Ryan ducks before driving a rear straight punch into the man's groin (2). Flowing forward, Ryan slips to the outside and grabs his opponent's neck and back to stabilize him (3). Next, he shifts his weight forward as he drives a series of knee thrusts into his foe's groin, ribs and solar plexus (4).

Boxing is a great place to start, but it shouldn't be your only field of study. It teaches great fundamentals—the jab, cross, hook and uppercut, as well as movement and evasion—and they're invaluable skills for reality fighting. However, boxing is limited in that it's designed for a one-on-one standing encounter against an opponent who's playing by the same rules.

The recommended way to develop your hand skills is to learn boxing or kickboxing—note that kickboxing uses more tools and requires a larger skill set than boxing, but it's still limited—and apply its tools to RBF-type scenarios. Real-word striking should encompass using all parts of your body, including your head, forearms, palms, elbows, fists, feet and knees. Furthermore, you should think of striking in its most liberal sense, which means it includes surgical attacks such as finger strikes to the eyes and gouges aimed at other vulnerable targets.

It's essential to practice striking back when you're in a variety of positions; standing is just one of them. Learn how to hit while you're on your back, on one knee and sitting in a chair. Experiment with every position you can think of.

One more observation about striking: Like everything in the martial arts, not all striking is created equal. Although everybody and his brother has a theory about how to hit with the greatest force, you'll do well to steer clear of the more esoteric methods. Stick to techniques that have been proved. If your instructor cannot demonstrate his theory of the ultimate power punch, maybe you should move on. Try to find one who understands the physics behind striking and who can explain it in scientific terms that make sense.

3) Learn Contact-and-Control Skills

Fighting is often a collision of energy, bodies hurtling at one another as force slams into force. That can take the form of a fist or foot smashing into an attacker's head, in which case the collision is controlled and confined to a specific body part. But just as often, people end up in body-to-body contact, which makes striking skills much more difficult. That's why you need to know grappling.

The best way to acquire basic grappling skills is to enroll in a wrestling or submission-grappling program. But beware: The problem with grappling is that it's a complex skill set. There are moves for besting an opponent from virtually any position and moves that will get you out of all of them while allowing you to submit him. That's precisely why you should avoid classes that teach an endless variety of submission holds. It can take a long time to become proficient at such an approach to grappling—which is fine as a physical pursuit but less than desirable for RBF. You need to acquire functional grappling skills quickly.

The next step is to delineate the initial goal of grappling with respect to RBF. In Dynamic Combat, this skill set is called "contact and control" for a reason: You want to exert control over any contact your opponent makes, from a wrist grab to a takedown followed by a full mount. A secondary goal is setting up a finishing technique. In any case, the mission is the same as it is with striking: to end the fight as quickly and effectively as possible.

Course of action: Skip the "15 ways to submit a person from the side mount" class, and focus on learning how to win the fight from whatever position you find yourself in. That often means doing everything you can to avoid fighting a grappling fight, sometimes by using strikes or other counterattacks. When you need to grapple, use it to extract yourself from a bad position and, ideally, maneuver until you're able to escape or strike. To that end, enroll in an MMA or *jiu-jitsu* course that permits striking—with protective gear, of course.

Photos by Thomas Sanders

LEARN CONTACT AND CONTROL: In reality-based fighting, technique is all about explosive movement and fluid action. Richard Ryan (right) and Tony Cortina face each other in a right lead (1). The opponent steps in with a lead jab, causing Ryan to move forward and drop his head below the punch as he deflects the strike upward and to the outside (2). Ryan uses his left guard hand to deflect the man's upper arm while driving his body weight forward and shooting his lead hand past his neck and head (3). Once he's inside the punch and has the arm trapped, Ryan directs his weight to the outside, executing a clothesline takedown (4). As the opponent falls, Ryan guides his head to the ground, palm-striking it several times (5). On a mat, this would have minimal effect, but on concrete, it would be devastating. By shifting his hips, Ryan can drop his weight onto the head and chest to finish the attacker (6).

4) LEARN THE PSYCHOLOGY OF FIGHTING

The fourth component of RBF is psychological; I refer to it as mind-set training. Without mental control, the rest of the 10 commandments will be useless.

Everyone has heard the adage that fighting is 90-percent mental and 10-percent physical. I think it's more like 50-50. It's true that without the mind, the body is useless, but the reverse is also true. The ancient Greeks got it right when they taught that to be effective, you need to have mind-body unity.

Mind-set training for RBF begins with learning how to manage fear under stress. Unless you do that, you won't be able to apply anything you've learned when you need it. You can learn fear management through self-study and visualization. Books, DVDs and the Internet are great resources. If you're looking for a place to start, do a Web search for Tony Blauer. His work often appears in the pages of *Black Belt* because he's a pioneer in the field of psychology as it pertains to self-defense.

5) LEARN WEAPONS

Another thing that makes RBF different from MMA is the weapons factor. Imagine what a cage fight would be like if one or both men had a knife or club. It would be ancient Rome all over again, and death would quickly follow. Because weapons are a given in a street fight, all good RBF programs include instruction in offensive and defensive methods.

Problem is, out of all the skill sets in the martial arts, weapons defense is the one that's least understood when it comes to reality fighting. Many instructors teach techniques that are likely to get their students killed. Examples: grabbing the knife hand of a slashing attacker or attempting to disarm a gunman from long range.

Photo by Thomas Sanders

Real-world weapons defense must include practical techniques and proven strategies that use timing, speed and deception to stack the deck in your favor. Unfortunately, such training is hard to find, especially when you want comprehensive coverage of the most common weapons.

In the real world, you have to be prepared for an attack from any type of weapon. Therefore, RBF training must encompass a full spectrum of possibilities. Again, it's not an easy task. The recommended source for instruction is law enforcement and the military.

IMPACT WEAPONS: Studying reality-based fighting isn't just about using different strikes and kicks; it's about using anything you have or can find to fight back. Assuming you're legally and morally justified, almost any object can become a survival tool.

10 COMMANDMENTS OF REALITY-BASED FIGHTING:
Step-by-Step Instructions for Transforming Yourself Into a Skilled Street Fighter
Part 2

by Richard Ryan • Black Belt October 2008

6) LEARN OFFENSIVE WEAPONS SKILLS

TO MANY PRACTITIONERS, the term "offensive weapons skills" connotes the moves that are used in traditional martial arts classes and tournaments—a spin with a *kama,* a block with a *tonfa* or a thrust with a *bo.* It's strange that the concept seldom goes beyond that, however, because since the dawn of time, weapons have been an integral part of combat training. Only in the modern era have they taken a back seat in the *dojo.*

The truth is, weapons training—when tethered with restraint, responsibility and an understanding of the law—is one of the most effective methods of personal protection. Weapons are the ultimate equalizer. Give a person a knife or a stick and a decent amount of instruction, and he'll be able to take on even a seasoned black belt and win. Skill with weapons offers an undeniable advantage in almost every situation.

Photos by Thomas Sanders

ARMED ATTACK: Self-defense against weapons requires specialized training because your actions must be based on the method of attack, range, type of weapon and other factors. To demonstrate, the opponent threatens Richard Ryan with a handgun, causing him to adopt a passive surrender posture (1). Ryan explodes forward and to the side of the weapon to get off the line of fire and simultaneously grabs the gun and the gun hand so he can deflect the barrel upward (2). If the gun discharges, it will be limited to the round in the chamber because Ryan's grip will stop the slide from cycling. Anticipating immediate withdrawal and resistance, Ryan moves forward along the attacker's centerline, twisting the barrel away from his head and body while delivering an elbow smash to the face (3). Continuing his line of motion, Ryan turns counterclockwise, wrenching the gun out of the opponent's grasp (4). He then uncoils from his loaded position and drives a hammerfist into the man's jaw or temple (5). Done correctly, the disarm should take no more than two seconds.

A good place to start is with a system such as *arnis* or *goshindo,* both of which can give you a working knowledge of how to handle various traditional fighting tools. But for the purposes of reality-based fighting, don't stop there. You most learn conventional and unconventional weaponry. A conventional weapon is something that's designed specifically to be a weapon and has no other purpose—for example, a handgun or an "assault rifle." In contrast, a kitchen knife, which can be as deadly as a *tanto,* is also an instrument used in food preparation. Therefore, it's classified as an un-conventional or expedient weapon. The category also includes everyday objects such as rocks, cell phones, pens and ashtrays—all of which can be converted into defensive devices.

Studying RBF requires you to master both types of weapons. Unfortunately, finding practical train-ing in such skills isn't easy. Do your homework before signing up with any instructor.

Footnote: Consider learning how to use a defensive firearm. The goal in RBF is to acquire the ability to fight; therefore, you should know how to fight with a gun. A variety of instructors and institutions offer excellent training. My state, Arizona, has Gunsite Training Center, the first such school to operate in the United States. I taught there for several years and can attest that it's worth the time and effort required to complete a course.

7) LEARN CRIME-PREVENTION STRATEGIES

If your training is to be used in real-world situations, it must include a study of practical applica-tions outside the dojo. This is where the line between martial arts and self-defense is blurred. Self-protection isn't just about fighting and the preparation for fighting; it's also about ways to avoid and prevent violence.

In this endeavor, an ounce of prevention truly is worth a pound of cure. The good news is that a great deal of information on crime awareness and prevention is available. Web sites, books and DVDs are the best places to begin. Also, check with your local police department to see whether it puts on crime-prevention seminars.

8) LEARN CONFRONTATION MANAGEMENT

Confrontation management has two parts: body language and verbal self-defense. Together, they'll help you defuse and de-escalate potentially violent situations while you prepare to fight back should it become necessary. These components, which to many seem diametrically opposed, represent a field that many martial arts instructors fail to address. Why? Primarily because confrontation management is a complex set of skills that require much knowledge and rehearsal to work.

The application of RBF skills in the real world often takes place in one of two situations: the sudden assault, in which you have no warning before you're forced to defend yourself; or the escalation, in which tension builds until violence erupts. It's the second scenario that can benefit from confrontation management. The trick lies in knowing how people act and react under stress.

Once again, you should begin your search for knowledge on the Internet. Although much of the information you'll find is based on resolving peaceful confrontations, some sources will tell you what to do if a problem gets physical. Look for courses that cover body language, nonverbal communica-tion, conflict negotiation and verbal self-defense. Of course, a good RBF instructor should be able to teach you the same material.

9) LEARN SITUATIONAL SURVIVAL SKILLS

In most martial arts schools, situational self-defense includes techniques for stopping common attacks such as being grabbed or jumped from behind. Some of the techniques are functional, especially if your attacker isn't too bright, but when you're preparing for the worst-case scenario, such static training is of limited value. You need to be more fluid and reactive.

The primary goal is to learn how to think on your feet in a variety of situations and positions. For example, I teach a form of training that forces students to apply their confrontation management and self-defense skills in situations in which a sudden attack is imminent. The key is to start slow and go through various attack and defense options before selecting the responses that are most effective and reaction-based.

Situational survival can also take the form of environmental training outside the dojo. Your first thought may be to find a park or other open space, but don't forget to also look for places that will force you to work in a confined environment under varying lighting conditions that mimic what you may encounter in the real world. Caution: Be smart and take extra precautions to preserve your safety and that of your partner. And remember that new drills will often present new hazards that must be addressed, perhaps with specialized protective gear.

Situational self-defense should also encompass extreme situations—fending off multiple opponents as well as multiple armed opponents. A good way to begin is to don protective gear and engage in controlled sparring matches in which two or more people attack you. Take it slow, controlling the speed and intensity until you and your partners have acquired enough skill to increase the tempo.

Photos by Thomas Sanders

GROUND FIGHTING: In RBF, fighting on the ground encompasses MMA-style grappling as well as no-rules striking and gouging. A single counterattack, properly placed with the right amount of energy, can end a violent encounter in a heartbeat (1). If such a technique isn't enough, however, the defender might have to employ a move that would never be allowed in competition— such as this thumb gouge to the eye (2).

10) LEARN ATTRIBUTE DEVELOPMENT

The final ingredient in the RBF recipe is you. A system is only as good as the person using it. Therefore, improving your attributes while minimizing any physical or mental liabilities you may have is the most important step in the journey to proficiency. You can learn all the technical skills in the world, but if you're out of shape and can't fight for 10 seconds, you'll be in trouble.

One of the biggest benefits of mixed-martial arts training is the work ethic it ingrains. Active sport fighters train much harder than most martial artists. That gives them a tremendous edge in any battle. Just as big lions usually eat little lions, healthy and strong lions usually dominate weak lions. That applies just as much to two-legged beings as it does to four-legged beings.

Developing your attributes is easy. Look for physical pursuits that will improve your speed, power and endurance, but remember that you also need to build your RBF conditioning, which means you have to get a little more specific in your training. Your goal should be to jump into a physical situation and maintain a sustained output for one minute. When that becomes easy, work up to three minutes. Bag work, sparring and reaction drills are great ways to get to that level.

YOUR PERSONAL RBF SYSTEM

The fastest way to develop proficiency at reality-based fighting is to seek out people and systems that specialize in this form of training because they will help you adapt the skills to your body. Some of the best instructors I've encountered are Walt Lysak Jr., Tony Blauer, Kelly S. Worden, Mike Lee Kanarek, Jim Wagner, Lamar M. Davis II, Paul Vunak, Kelly McCann and Avi Nardia.

Remember, however, that in the end, it's impossible to train for every situation you may encounter on the street. Attempting to do so would take many lifetimes, and even then, Murphy's law can come into play. Be selective about how you approach your training. Take the time to assess your personal attributes and liabilities: What are you good at, and what are you not good at? Start with your strengths and develop them first because they will help you develop the other skills.

As you seek out instruction, make sure that what you're learning fits in with the outline I've presented here. Then, once you've mastered the basics of a particular skill set or knowledge base, move on to the next one. If you later discover that you'd like more information about a certain subject because it interests you, feel free to focus on it.

At the end of the day, the road you take is up to you—and that's the way it should be. There is more than one path up the mountain, and the journey is more important than the destination. Last bit of advice: Training is essential, but knowledge is power. When it comes to reality-based fighting, the more you know, the greater your potential will be.

Photo by Thomas Sanders

STOPPING VIOLENCE: Doing what it takes to survive is the motto of reality martial arts. To stop a takedown, Richard Ryan uses his shield maneuver, coupled with an upward eye rake. Few attackers would feel like continuing the fight after such a painful, and potentially blinding, response.

ASSESSING THE BATTLEFIELD:
Developing the Observational Skills You Need for Reality-Based Self-Defense!

by Sammy Franco • Black Belt March 2009

IN SELF-DEFENSE, assessment refers to the rapid gathering of information and the subsequent evaluation of it to determine whether it represents a threat. Using perception and observation, you study people, places, objects and behaviors before you arrive at a quick conclusion and take action.

You gather information through your senses. You see motion in the shadows or hear footsteps behind you. You smell cigarette smoke in what you thought was a deserted area. You feel a breeze coming up the stairwell when all the doors and windows are supposed to be shut.

As useful as the five senses naturally are, they can be sharpened using exercises designed to develop detection and identification capabilities. For example, sit alone in your backyard and catalog the things your senses lock onto. Next, list the possible sources of the data. At first, you might find it difficult to make connections, but with practice, you'll be able to quickly identify the sources. Run through the exercise in different settings and you'll heighten your abilities even more. For example, imagine the things you'd hear, see and smell at night in the middle of a suburban park, as opposed to what you'd experience standing in a dark alley.

Fortunately, you can bolster your ability to observe when you need to. Have you ever noticed how keenly you study people, buildings, street signs, animals and other everyday things when you travel to a strange city? People tend to pay closer attention in new environments and become less observant in familiar settings.

Photo courtesy of Sammy Franco

For students of self-defense, assessment means rapidly gathering and analyzing information, then accurately evaluating it in terms of the danger it might represent.

CHOOSING YOUR RESPONSE

Accurate assessment is critical for choosing the most appropriate tactical response to an attack, which is why you have five options:

1. To comply is to do what the assailant commands. If you're held at gunpoint outside of disarming range, there's no option but to comply.
2. To escape is also known as the tactical retreat. You flee from the threat safely and rapidly.
3. To de-escalate or defuse a hostile situation is an art and a science, but it's an essential skill because not every confrontation warrants fighting back. Often, you'll be able to talk someone out of using violence to get what he wants.

4. To assert effective communication skills can enable you to thwart a person's efforts to intimidate, dominate and control you. For example, you're working late at the office and your boss makes sexual advances toward you. In a firm and confident manner, you tell him that you're not interested and that you want him to stop immediately.

5. To fight back entails using physical and psychological tactics and techniques to stun, incapacitate or kill the attacker.

AVOIDING EXCESSIVE FORCE

Assessment also enables you to avoid trouble with the law. The more skilled you are with firearms, knives, sticks or your empty hands, the higher the standard of care that you must observe when protecting yourself or others. If you act too quickly or use excessive force when neutralizing an assailant, you may end up in court.

The two most popular questions students ask after they've learned a little self-defense are, "When can I use physical force?" and "How much force is justified?" There are no simple answers because every situation is different. In one case, a side kick that dislocates an attacker's knee might be judged appropriate. Change the facts a little, and you'll find yourself facing a civil lawsuit or criminal charges. That's why it's important to properly assess a situation and, if possible, avoid violence altogether.

De-escalation is the process of strategically defusing a potentially violent confrontation. The goal is to eliminate the possibility of an agitated individual resorting to violence. You must use verbal and nonverbal techniques to calm him while employing tactically deceptive physical safeguards to create the appearance that you are nonaggressive.

USING YOUR SKILLS

The best way to ensure that you can read potentially dangerous situations is to always be alert. Don't become complacent and comfortable. Assess the situation promptly and accurately, then form a rational conclusion and choose the appropriate tactical response.

The only time assessment doesn't play a role is when you're attacked by surprise. If a mugger lunges from behind a car, grabs you by the throat and throws you to the ground, it's too late to assess anything. You must act intuitively and immediately to neutralize him, or you'll be a statistic.

Assuming you have time to assess a situation, you should focus your attention on two areas: the environment and the individual(s). Your environment includes four components in your immediate surroundings.

Find an escape route. There's nothing cowardly about running away from a dangerous situation because the ultimate goal of self-defense is to survive. Scan your environment for windows, doors, fire escapes, gates, escalators, fences, walls, bridges and staircases. Make sure that your "escape route" doesn't lead you into a worse situation.

Locate barriers or any object that obstructs the attacker's path to you. At the very least, barriers give you distance and time. They must have the structural integrity to perform the function you've assigned

Photo courtesy of Sammy Franco

them. Common barriers include desks, doors, automobiles, dumpsters, large trees, fences, walls and vending machines.

Makeshift weapons using everyday objects can be viable tools as long as the one you choose can do what you need it to do. For example, you won't be able to knock out a thug with a car antenna, but you can whip it across his eyes and temporarily blind him. A heavy flashlight, however, will enable you to KO an assailant rather easily.

Know the terrain. You must determine the strategic implications of the terrain you're on. Will the surface interfere with your ability to defend yourself? Is the ground wet or dry? If you're standing on ice, for instance, your escape and kicking options are limited.

The ability to assess a threat includes having situational awareness. You must be alert, present and focused on virtually everything in your vicinity. You must train your senses to detect people, places, objects and actions that can harm you.

EVALUATING THE THREAT

Perhaps the most difficult part of assessment is determining how much of a threat a person represents. You must pay attention to all the clues. Let your senses absorb the necessary information and don't forget to listen to what your instincts tell you and follow the five factors warrant consideration.

Note the person's demeanor or behavior. Is he shaking or calm and calculated? Are his shoulders hunched or relaxed? Are his hands clenched? Is he breathing hard? Is he angry or frustrated, or confused and scared? Does he seem high on drugs, mentally ill or intoxicated? Is his speech slurred? What is his tone of voice? Is he talking rapidly or methodically? Is he cursing and angry? All these cues are essential in evaluating his demeanor and thus selecting the right response.

Once you've observed his demeanor, you're in a better position to assess his intent. What's his

One of the most important lessons for assessing an enemy: If you cannot see his hands, be cautious because he could be concealing a weapon.

purpose in confronting you? Does he intend to rob you? Is he seeking retribution for something you've done, or is he simply looking to pick a fight? Note that when it comes to criminals, intent can change quickly—an encounter that starts as a robbery can quickly escalate to a murder.

In real-world self-defense, there are three distances or range from which your assailant can attack: kicking, punching and grappling. While you assess a threat, note the strategic implications of the distance between you and him. Is he close enough to kick? Is he within arm's reach, which means punching and grappling are possible? Is he moving through the ranges, and if so, how quickly? Does he continue to advance when you step back?

Find the spatial relationship of the assailant(s) to you in terms of threat, escape and target selection. Are you surrounded by multiple assailants, or is there only one attacker? Is he standing squarely or sideways? What anatomical targets does he present? Is he blocking the door? Is he close to something you'd like to use as a makeshift weapon?

Note if the assailant has a weapon. Is the assailant armed or unarmed? If he has a weapon, does he have a delivery method for it? Does he have more than one weapon? Sometimes it's easy to determine whether a person is armed—for example, you see a knife sheath on his belt. At other times, you need to be more attentive. If he's wearing a jacket when it's too hot for a jacket, he could be concealing a gun. If he has one hand behind his body or in a pocket, he might be reaching for a knife. As I teach in my system, Contemporary Fighting Arts, anytime you're uncertain if your opponent has a weapon, always assume that he's armed. It may be the last item on the list of things to look for when you're assessing a potential threat, but it will shape everything you do and say.

COMPETITION VS. DESTRUCTION:
Reality Fighting's Cardinal Rule—
Train Your Brain!

by Tim Larkin and Chris Ranck-Buhr • Black Belt September 2007

LAS VEGAS—TWO THUGS ambush a well-known *jiu-jitsu* competitor in a casino parking lot. Without a second thought, he lunges and deftly executes a double-leg takedown on the first guy. The man is knocked unconscious when his head strikes a car door on the way down.

The second assailant comes at the jiu-jitsu competitor with a knife. He parries the blade and immobilizes the limb with an armbar. The man shrieks in agony and begins slapping his thigh with his free hand to signal his submission. The jiu-jitsu practitioner lets him go, and without missing a beat, the thug recovers and drives his blade hilt deep into the martial artist's torso again and again.

The jiu-jitsu expert survives the attack, but he's not unscathed. His injuries force him to retire from competition, and to this day, he still suffers from digestive problems.

What went wrong? Was the competitor simply outclassed? Is there any truth to the conventional wisdom that street thugs are simply better fighters? Hardly. The difference is more subtle than that. It's not about technique or training; it's about the ultimate goal each man had in mind.

The jiu-jitsu competitor was performing the way he'd practiced, but then so was the thug. While their two methods of handling the situation can be seen as similar—the armbar and the stab are, in essence, martial arts techniques—their goals were not. One man was pitting skill against skill and strength against strength, while the other was simply wrecking human tissue.

One was thinking competition, while the other was bent on destruction.

Photo by Rick Hustead

NO MERCY: As soon as he detects a threat—in this case, a concealed weapon about to be deployed—Tim Larkin (right) closes the gap, slams his left forearm into the assailant's neck and punches him in the ribs.

WHAT ARE YOU TRAINING FOR?

We'd all like to believe that our martial arts training prepares us for every possible situation in and out of the ring, but often that's not the case. Numerous true stories with unfortunate outcomes could be told about competitors who faced raw violence on the street. To save yourself from having a sad story of your own, you have to be honest: What are you training for? Is it to best a martial artist in the ring, to score points, to win a trophy? Or is it to break people, to render them harmless as soon as they threaten your well-being? Do you understand the difference?

Competition is about seeing who's best among relative equals, while violence is about shutting off a human brain. In the first endeavor, the goal is to determine who can apply the tools in his bag of tricks in the most cunning way, while in the other, it's to find the unfair advantage and exploit it.

Competition entails using your body and mind to play chess at 90 miles per hour. It involves pitting your strength, speed, stamina, drive and skill against your opponent's attributes to decide who will be the victor and who will be the vanquished.

Violence is about one human being destroying another. It's a baseball bat to the back of the head. It's three ganging up on one. It's kicking an attacker when he's down, especially when he's down. While there can be such a thing as a fair fight, there's no such thing as an equitable murder.

GUN: The assailant points his weapon at Tim Larkin's chest (1). Larkin steps forward with his right foot to remove his body from the line of fire (2) and shoulder-butts the man's chest as he controls his right arm (3). The martial artist then leverages the opponent to the ground (4), strikes him in the groin (5) and punches him in the throat (6).

COMPETITOR VS. KILLER

The difference between a sparring match and a murder is as simple to understand as the difference between wrestling and shooting people. In wrestling, trained practitioners in the same weight class have a roughly equal chance; in a shooting, a bullet destroys regardless of the victim's physical prowess or skill.

In a wrestling match, even with the most vicious and painful joint lock, you're not going to ruin body parts. You're not going to break your opponent's elbow; you're going to make him feel like it's breaking to make him submit.

The killer is much more interested in duplicating, by any means available, the work of the bullet. He simply wants to destroy parts of you until you don't function anymore. He knows that outside the ring, the only rules are the laws of physics.

He's not interested in a fair fight to make you submit; he's going to start in on you when you're not looking and when you least expect it. He wants to injure you, grievously and permanently, and he won't stop until he's succeeded. In his mind, the best way to get that done is to make sure you never get a say in what he's going to do—no countering, no blocking, in short, no competition. He wants to keep it as one-sided as possible.

In competition, both parties step into the ring and know what to expect. They have a good grasp of what their opponent is capable of and probably have worked out strategies to best him. They know that if things go badly, they have friends—the referee or a cornerman with a towel—who will call it off. They know that no matter what, they have to worry about only one guy. They know no one's going to dig their eyeballs out of their skull or break their neck or pull a snub-nose .38 out of their pocket.

Photos by Rick Hustead

REAR CHOKE: As soon as the assailant initiates his attack (1), Tim Larkin effects a groin grab with his left hand (2). He turns his torso to the left to relieve pressure on his neck until the pain of the groin lift breaks the chokehold (3). Larkin then pivots, drops to one knee and forces the opponent down (4). After accosting him with a "back breaker," Larkin shoves the man to the ground (5) and hammerfists his body and head (6).

Dennis Rader, the notorious BTK killer, reveled in taking on multiple people at once—whole families, single-handedly—and succeeded with no training and no special skill. He wasn't interested in fighting or competing with his victims on a physical level. He simply wanted to kill them.

How could he do that? Because he's not a fighter; he's a killer. Fighters do their best to out-compete their foes; killers do their best to avoid competition. They find or manufacture the unfair advantage and exploit it mercilessly.

The defining difference between the competitor and the killer comes down to injury. The desire to inflict a serious injury that requires immediate medical attention for the most part isn't a goal in competition. When it does occur, it ends the match instantly. The ref jumps in, the cornerman throws in the towel and everyone piles into the ring to administer first aid.

In violence, the goal is injury. That's because, on the street as in the ring, injury ends all competition.

DYING TO COMPETE WITH VIOLENCE

The real danger arises when you try to push competition into the realm of violence. Competing with a killer, trying to "play by the rules" while he knows there aren't any, will get you killed. Put him in an armbar, and he'll tap out; as soon as you let up, he'll stab you.

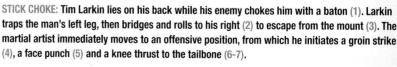

STICK CHOKE: Tim Larkin lies on his back while his enemy chokes him with a baton (1). Larkin traps the man's left leg, then bridges and rolls to his right (2) to escape from the mount (3). The martial artist immediately moves to an offensive position, from which he initiates a groin strike (4), a face punch (5) and a knee thrust to the tailbone (6-7).

Martial artists need to learn to keep competition out of violence, to maintain a clear delineation between what happens in the ring and what happens on the street. In the ring, the best man wins; on the street, the one who relentlessly destroys the other prevails.

The secret to success on the street is simple—and at times gruesome. Break the arm, rupture the testicles, stomp the throat. Do all the things that are expressly forbidden in competition, and do them first. The fancier the technique you're monkeying around with and the longer the setup, the more danger you expose yourself to.

Everything changes in your favor when you jam your thumb in your attacker's eye. It's not nice and it's not fair, but it will prevent him from having the chance to do the same to you.

ONE OR THE OTHER?

While it would be nice to say that you can train for the ring and the street, you can't. It's a simple fact that you'll do what you train to do—as the jiu-jitsu competitor in the aforementioned Las Vegas assault did. Keeping two kinds of training, with their vastly different goals, separated in your head just doesn't work.

Many of the skills and techniques you can amass by competing in martial arts tournaments can translate to the street—a choke is a choke, after all—but the methodologies under which they're practiced and executed differ. In the ring, you can wrap him up without worrying that he'll pull a blade. On the street, you're better off injuring him before you go for the choke.

Figure out what your goal is. If you want to be a hard target and know how to shut people off on the street, make sure your training reflects that. If you want to compete, keep it in the ring and enjoy the physical and mental challenges that the sport provides.

TRAINING FOR LONGEVITY

For most people, however, competition is but a short phase of their total athletic career. Sooner or later, your "war wounds" will stack up, the mutant healing powers of youth will abandon you and you'll have achieved all your competitive goals. That's the time to switch over to destruction training. Your body's ability to handle the rigors of competition has a built-in fuse; the harder you drive yourself, the more ends you're burning it from. Destruction, on the other hand, is a life skill that will see you through to the end of your days—by making sure you get as many days as you can.

THE SPEAR:
Tony Blauer's Latest Discovery
May Turn the Martial Arts World Upside-Down
Part 1

Interview by Robert W. Young • Black Belt March 2000

BACK IN 1982, a decade before the Ultimate Fighting Championship and years before other reality-based-combat simulations, Tony Blauer created the "panic attack," a training drill that accounted for the way a real-life adrenaline dump affects a martial artist's breathing, focus and complex motor skills. He discovered what everyone else found out once the UFC burst onto the scene: Theory and practice are not the same.

Black Belt: The result of your latest research is called the SPEAR. What does that mean?

Tony Blauer: SPEAR is an acronym for Spontaneous Protection Enabling Accelerated Response. Understanding the theory behind the acronym is the first step in understanding how and why many self-defense systems are predisposed to fail in a real, sudden, violent assault.

BB: Why do you think most self-defense systems will fail?

Blauer: Most of what martial artists practice is not real. The moment there is consent, there is awareness—which means there is preparation. These psychological components completely change your mind-set. In a real situation, there are so many emotional and psychological factors that the sensory overload can negate all those years of training. The remedy is to address the problem of how real fights occur and what is behaviorally realistic. In other words, you must proactively analyze how you are likely to move and think in a real assault and train around that model.

BB: Is that what your system does?

Blauer: My system focuses on "adversity drills." We are always working on recovery principles.

WRONG WAY TO RESPOND: As a verbal confrontation begins, the stress builds and the defender (right) may experience an adrenaline dump (1). When the attack is initiated (2), the defender flinches (3). When his arms instinctively come up to protect his head, the attacker can easily land his blow (4).

Most people focus on the offensive, not the protective. In other words, most people tend to fixate on what they will do to the opponent, not what their opponent will try to do to them. This slight perspective shift is the difference between a proactive training session that increases perception speed and decreases reaction time. And that's a fundamental difference. Our focus is on a simple three-tiered premise that seems to elude most self-defense curricula: One, real fights are not fun. Two, real fights are technically messy. Three, real fights are those confrontations in which emotionally we wish we were somewhere else.

BB: How does the SPEAR fit in?

Blauer: The SPEAR is genetically inspired and intuitively engineered. Our true survival system in concert with our intellect, experience and instincts can combine to enhance safety if we don't botch it by learning contradictory muscle-memory sequences or wiring presumptuous decision-making programs. Behaviorally speaking, we all move away from danger, but tactically the only way to stop a close-quarters physical threat is by moving *toward* the threat. Real fights happen inside the space of a phone booth.

BB: And the SPEAR addresses this?

Blauer: Yes, the SPEAR is the only behaviorally based self-defense system that analyzes and uses the survival flinch spawned through a survival/startle mechanism in the brain. In a true ambush moment, your brain experiences a delay between stimulus and response. In reality, it's not a response; it's a reaction. This is the paradox of martial arts training. When we agree to fight, we can mentally adjust and respond. But when the attack is a true surprise, we are more likely to react rather than respond.

BB: How does the SPEAR use the body's natural reactions?

Blauer: Over the past 20 years, I've analyzed the most common responses to surprises and designed cognitive drills around them. Methodical practice of these tactics turns your natural flinch into a trigger to engage your close-quarters arsenal. In other words, it helps you convert a genetically supported reactive response to a real threat into a protective action. You learn to move from a reactive state to make a responsive statement. I have not invented a new style; I have created a realistic and effective bridge so you get to the style you are trained in. If you lose it in that initial contact moment, it may be too late to recover.

BB: For years, you have been on a quest to learn exactly what happens in a real fight, and now that path has led to the SPEAR. How did it begin?

Blauer: In 1986 and 1987 I developed the sucker-punch drill. I wore only a mouth guard for protection, and my training partner wore 16-ounce gloves. I was not allowed to strike; I could only evade and avoid. The drill always started with dialogue at close quarters, and I had to maintain that close proximity while trying to verbally defuse it.

BB: Did that drill develop from your trademark panic-attack drill?

Blauer: Yes. It's important to understand the evolution and progression. There were a few groups out

RIGHT WAY TO RESPOND: Using Tony Blauer's SPEAR system, the defender (right) can convert his body's natural reactions into a protective tactic. As the punch begins (1-2), the defender moves forward to intercept it before it attains maximum power (3). Once the defender has nullified the attack, he is in position to follow up with a close-quarters technique (4).

there trying to push the envelope. They were sparring hard and doing multiple-assailant drills. Some were wearing gear, but there was always something missing: real-time evolving dialogue and reciprocal risk. In other words, once the fight started, both the role-player and the defender had equal opportunity.

BB: How is that different from the sucker-punch drill and the SPEAR?

Blauer: If you spar hard or against several opponents, it's still sparring and there's still the [aspect of] consent and awareness. If you are doing scenarios and only one person attacks, there is no real risk. The adrenaline dump is created by performance anxiety, not a potential threat or the fear of failure. Many people, especially some of the newer groups doing simulations, do not completely grasp this. And those two components are the missing ingredients in a real dynamic simulation where a true "emotional blueprint" is created. If there is no dialogue and no unpredictable risk for both parties, the simulation is partial. You can't jump in a swimming pool and wrestle with a rubber shark and then believe you're ready to handle "jaws." And that insight is why the panic attack is uniquely different from many simulation systems. Our effort to develop attack-specific responses within scenario-specific simulations is why the sucker-punch drill was developed. I wanted to create a close-quarters isolation drill to address the sudden attack.

BB: Why is scenario-specific training so important?

Blauer: Because scenario-specific training is the only process that can mature and develop the body/mind connection.

The versatility of the SPEAR allows it to be used to defend against a realistic attack such as a tackle. To illustrate, Tony Blauer (right) simply lowers his center of gravity to jam a charging grappler.

And it develops the pre-contact stage, the missing link in all training. Sparring, no matter how you do it, is still just sparring. It is not scenario-specific, and there's a huge difference between attack-specific training and scenario-specific training. Attack-specific is when you work on how to get out of a choke or how to get out of a multiple-assailant situation. Scenario-specific is about the situation and how you got there. It induces a different adrenaline state; and most important, it creates the mental blueprint that can heighten your awareness in a real-life confrontation.

BB: How are surprise attacks related to the SPEAR?

Blauer: Everybody forgets that in a real attack, you are somewhere doing something else, not waiting for someone to signal the start of the fight. Predators look for victims they can surprise. In real life, you don't know when or where someone's going to hit you. After creating the panic-attack system, I wanted to be able to refine special moments in a conflict. We had verbal-assault drills and pain-management drills, and I wanted a sucker-punch drill since that big right hand was common and fairly predictable. Embracing all I had learned in the role-playing panic attacks, the sucker-punch drill was pretty obvious. Phase one would start with a hostile verbal exchange that was escalating. The conversation was crucial to the success of the adrenaline dump and the element of surprise. I refer to this principle as adversity training—creating drills where the probability of failure was greater than the probability of success. Too many martial artists spend most of their time worrying about looking good rather than recovering from a Murphy moment.

BB: Anyhow, we'd be in a heated verbal exchange, and even though I knew one punch was coming, I didn't know when or where. It could be a punch to my groin, a shot to my bladder, an uppercut or an overhand. I found that once the adrenal system kicked in, the first thing to go was breath control and lucid verbal skills. Hyperventilation compromises blood flow to the brain. That's a problem if you want to think clearly. That is the magic of a truly behaviorally based approach.

Blauer: The sucker-punch drill messed with all the notions of control and focus. I had to proactively design verbal defusing and distraction segues for real assaults: What can I say if I am being mugged? What can I say if am at an ATM or in my car? Years later, I was explaining the process to a researcher in Texas who develops nutritional supplements, and he called it a genetically inspired self-defense system. He said I was wiring into the tactics that the human survival system wants to do, whereas other martial arts are based on learning and muscle memory.

BB: How did that evolve into the SPEAR?

Blauer: With the sucker-punch drill, I was trying to use a physical tactic

Tony Blauer (right) uses the tactical SPEAR to intercept a roundhouse kick. As he charges inside the attacker's defense and positions himself too close to be kicked, he can easily disrupt the other man's balance.

when I had no knowledge of where my opponent's attack would originate. Because the sequential relationship of the martial arts has no basis in reality, I got hit. That's because most tactics are based on your anticipation of a specific physical attack. The drill totally changed all that. Here's the most important aspect for instructors: I could've changed the drill because I was failing, but I didn't. I wanted to understand why my training didn't support this.

BB: What conclusions did you arrive at after studying the outcome of that drill?

Blauer: A couple times I completely escaped the moment of impact by flinching. As I flinched, my shoulder would come up, and my hands would protect my face. Or I'd duck. I realized that flinch speed, which is born of your survival system picking up the danger, is faster than cognitive speed. The body is genetically wired to survive. We slow it down by saying, "My style says I should do this," because that thinking process requires us to identify the attack and then diagnose it before treating it.

BB: Why don't more people realize that?

Blauer: Because most martial arts training is done through imitation. And most of it is codified. The paradox is that we're taught to maintain or create distance and then engage the other person in calculated movements. We teach people to spar to prepare for a real street fight, and that's wrong. You should be able to turn into the creature from *Alien*: Get in the guy's face, knock him on his butt, give him a rebirthing experience so he's flashing back to being in his mother's womb and forgetting that he's a serial killer or a violent mugger. Maybe that's a little dramatic, but the potential must be there. The only way to reverse the predator/prey relationship is to make the predator pray.

STUDENTS OF THE SPEAR

In case you're wondering just how legitimate Tony Blauer's SPEAR system really is, check out this partial list of agencies that have paid big bucks to learn it:

- **Australian Federal Police**
- **Dallas (Texas) Police Department**
- **Federal Air Marshals**
- **Federal Bureau of Investigation**
- **Houston (Texas) Police Department SWAT Unit**
- **Illinois State Police**
- **Rochester (New York) Police Department**
- **Tampa (Florida) Police Department**
- **U.S. Coast Guard**
- **U.S. Department of Defense**

THE SPEAR:
Tony Blauer's Latest Discovery
May Turn the Martial Arts World Upside Down
Part 2

Interview by Robert W. Young • Black Belt April 2000

BLACK BELT: You mentioned phase one of the sucker-punch drill; what other phases were involved?

Tony Blauer: The drill evolved so my partner could do as many shots as he wanted. Phase two had two strikes, phase three had three, and so on. From this drill, the SPEAR system was born. It teaches us to convert flinching into tactics. It also addresses the paradox of moving away from a threat rather than engaging it.

BB: Explain how the drill developed.

Blauer: The only way I could control my partner was by moving toward him and jamming him. If I tried to block, parry or evade, I got nailed during phase three and up. There's no way to not get hit if you maintain a distance where you allow your opponent to reload—another missing link and paradox of standard training. Because of the unpredictability of the attack, my initial move was a flinch. Performance ego demanded that I try various moves from my theoretical/cognitive arsenal. They usually failed. So quickly I recognized that flinching speed, triggered by unconscious neuromuscular communication, was much faster than conscious neuromuscular communication. I then created drills that were attached to the primal, midbrain responses. In time, I learned how to trigger my cognitive brain as I flinched. It allowed me to move toward the threat sooner. Again, the behavioral paradox is that when we are in danger, we want to move away, but the tactical directive is to move in.

BB: So the SPEAR capitalizes on the flinch reflex?

Blauer: The flinch is the foundation and spark of the SPEAR. Our close-quarters arsenal is based on this conversion process. It's based on an instinctive single-mindedness for the survival system to protect the command center: the head. Consider this: A guy gets punched and goes down. He may be getting kicked in the stomach, but his hands will still be covering his head. He's not moving his arms or covering the parts of his body that get hit. Whenever you are blitz-attacked and not sure what's happening, your hands come up. Irrespective of your training, if a stimulus is introduced too quickly, you will flinch.

BB: What is the physiological purpose of flinching?

Blauer: It's the physical response to an emotional startle where we intuit a physical threat. The flinch is designed

Tony Blauer (bottom) uses the SPEAR system to block a punch thrown at him during a ground attack.

to protect the body's command center: the eyes, ears, throat and brain. When you realize you're in danger, the flinch happens. For those on a path of self-discovery or looking for a realistic survival system, it's imperative to appreciate and incorporate the flinch mechanism. It takes courage because you need to consider the conflict of contemporary training methods. In sparring, you're taught to step back. You're actually moving into the trajectory of the attack because the attacker is always a step ahead of you in an ambush-type assault. The real fight is when you're ambushed, not when you're the sniper.

BB: Did you modify the flinch, or do you just go off whatever comes naturally?

Blauer: Through thousands of evaluations of how people move and from research that involved talking with people who were attacked, I was able to identify three [kinds of] flinches that are triggered by proximity sense and angle of attack. If somebody suddenly charges at you from a distance, the flinch is to widen your power base and thrust your hands out to push away the danger. If someone comes running at you with a machete or a baseball bat, you don't run toward him. People think they'll run away, but running is not an immediate primal response. Hesitation, freezing and denial are the common behavioral responses. Then the fight-or-flight syndrome might kick in, but in real life, it's more like the fight-flight-or-freeze syndrome because people often hesitate when they should jump out of the way.

BB: What's the second type of flinch?

Blauer: The second one is from striking range. Somebody comes at you from just outside arm's reach—for example, while you're having a verbal confrontation over a coveted parking spot, the guy lunges. Is it a shove, a choke or a hook punch? Who knows? Who can actually see it at that moment and distance? And here's the point: Your reactive brain just screams "Look out!" and voilà, flinch No. 2. Your hands come up to protect your head, your weight gets transferred to your back leg, you close your eyes and you turn away from the danger.

FLINCH VS. KICKING ATTACK: As the attacker prepares to deliver a kick to the head, Tony Blauer positions his arms to intercept the leg (1). Blauer then thrusts his arms into the attacker's shins before the kick can attain maximum power (2).

BB: And the third type?

Blauer: The third is similar to version two, but the angle is more severe because the threat is much closer. In this flinch, you do what I call a shielding action in which you actually cover your head with an arm. It's like holding a medieval shield against your forearm as you block and strike. From that shielding position, you kind of twist or "corkscrew" away from the attack.

BB: How does the flinch manifest itself in combat?

Blauer: Well, this brings us back to the contradiction of athletic performance-based trained versus adversity drills and trying to replicate the conditions that'll be present in a real assault. Here's a metaphor: Look at the patriotic war films that came out after World War I and II, then look at *Saving Private Ryan.* It's fantasy versus fact. The SPEAR system is about proactively analyzing fact and creating the most realistic "fake" drills we can. So when real-life conflicts happen, your adaptation challenge is minimal. Here's a graphic example that relates to the frustration of classical training and how a reactive response triggered by a real-life assault can short-circuit your whole theoretical arsenal. Often, a murdered police officer will have defensive wounds on the hands: bullet holes or knife slashes. The assumption is that the officer was trying to wrestle for the weapon. I disagree. Those wounds do not come from trying to grab the weapon. They come from flinching. When you grab, you grab toward the wrist or along the side of the weapon—not at the tip of the knife or gun. Those incidents most likely happen like this: The cop is chasing a suspect, who pulls out a gun and turns quickly. The cop flinches. He doesn't parry the weapon like he was taught. His hands come up in front of his face.

BB: Is the first step in learning the SPEAR simply accepting that we all flinch?

Blauer: Yes. By accepting the flinch, two things occur. First, you realize that it's a survival mechanism that you will do whether you like it or not. Second, you realize that the fastest thing you can do is work off the flinch. Ask anybody who's been in a real explosive fight what the first thing he threw was, and he'll say: "I don't know. It happened so fast. The next thing I knew I was drilling the guy in the head."

BB: Has that happened to you?

Blauer: In the first big fight I can remember, a guy winged a punch at me while I was talking to him. My hands naturally came up to protect my head, and they deflected his punch. Because he threw it so hard, he was jammed against me in a spontaneous clinch, so I just grabbed his head and shoulder and did a hip throw. He fell because of how the flinch intercepted his haymaker—not because I stepped in, caught his arm and executed a judo throw.

FLINCH VS. STRIKING ATTACK: If he is lying on his back, Tony Blauer can use the SPEAR to stop a punch. Once he detects the incoming blow, Blauer readies his arms (1). He makes contact with the attacker's biceps area because it moves more slowly than the fist and imparts less force (2).

BB: Did you use any formal martial arts techniques?

Blauer: Because I'd had a huge adrenaline dump, my next move was certainly not a fine-motor skill like "the third metacarpal bone must be twisted this way." He was on his butt trying to get up, but he was winded from the fall. I grabbed him by the hair and threw him into the furniture right beside us. Again, it was spontaneous gross-motor tactics.

BB: How hard is it for the average martial artist to learn how to work off the flinch in a natural way?

Blauer: Not hard. The SPEAR is truly a genetically inspired system. This means the foundation isn't something you have to learn. It is built on unique drills that coordinate the instincts and body mechanics that human beings are all born with. It is easy to get started with the SPEAR, and it's actually easier for a layperson to learn than for an instructor to teach—as paradoxical as that may seem. But if you just scratch the surface, you will miss the best of it. And if you look at it once and never look back, you'll only be exposed to the stuff I developed yesterday—which is good, but it's constantly getting better. If I had developed my system in the 1960s and then stopped researching, the foundation would still have been sound. But the trends and issues of surviving today are different from those we had to be concerned with back then.

BB: Is it a matter of just listening to an audiotape or watching a videotape, or does a martial artist actually have to do some kind of drills?

Blauer: It's a combination. You could just listen to the tapes and start incorporating the principles. They're that natural. Remember that it's easy to learn because it's based on how the body actually moves, not on how some animal moves or on reconfiguring your body to acquire a new muscle

FLINCH VS. KICKING ATTACK: The SPEAR allows martial artists to use their body's natural response to an attack to protect themselves (1-2). After neutralizing the immediate threat, they can deliver a knee thrust or any other technique taught in their martial art (3).

memory. It's based on spontaneity. There are also drills to develop it. One of the ones I created is called the "range rover"; it takes you out of the driver's seat and puts your training partner in control of your arsenal. A chess master once said that the height of strategy is not doing your best move, but doing the worst move for your opponent. Yet people are always practicing their best move and they try to use it all the time. They should be looking at where their opponent is open or where he doesn't think he's going to get hit because that's tactically the best thing you could do to hurt him physically and psychologically.

BB: In a fight, do you flinch and then think about how you can strike, or do you actually modify your flinch into an attack?

Blauer: It should be both. It depends on what the bad guy's doing and how much homework you've done. You could say to yourself, "I'm going to hit him from where I flinch." Because flinching is so primal, it actually locks and loads your most dangerous close-quarters weapons: elbow strikes, eye rakes, head butts, eye gouges and so on.

BB: Exactly when in a fight do you initiate the SPEAR?

Blauer: The SPEAR is the conversion, so anything you do right from a flinch is a SPEAR. Many people misinterpret the SPEAR as the physical move I often demo in which contact is made with my forearms. But since the flinch is triggered by the aggression of the opponent, you may find yourself flinching away and side-kicking while leaning over a chair in a bar. If you throw the kick without worrying about repositioning to get in your stance, you have "SPEARed" your opponent because you struck from where you were and *spontaneously protected* yourself. And the startle/flinch combo *enabled accelerated response.*

BB: How does this strategy tie in with the skills martial artists already possess?

Blauer: If you're a boxer and somebody sucker-punches you on the street, you will flinch. If you incorporate the SPEAR, you can engage the attacker and then disengage using the SPEAR system to set up your uppercut. If you're a Thai boxer and you are jumped at an ATM, you won't go into a neck hookup and a knee thrust; you will protect yourself first by flinching. The SPEAR nails the person as he's moving in and creates space. Suddenly, you get a chance to throw that knee strike or shin kick. If you're a *taekwondo* player, it's the same. If I'm a foot away from you in a bar and I start something, you won't be able to do a jump back kick or side kick. But you will flinch. And if you can hit me from the flinch using the SPEAR, that's good for you. You can use your flinch, which at that range and in that context is faster than anything else, as an impetus to get tactical.

BB: How does the SPEAR work physically?

Blauer: The common SPEAR is to use the forearms. This is more natural because of our instinct to cover our head by raising our arms. Getting students to engage the attacker—to actually move toward the bad guy—is a challenge. So the tactical SPEAR demands that we engage the threat. Our movement is like an impaling, penetrating tool. It's not a block; like a traditional spear, it moves in for the attack. The physical evolution of the SPEAR went like this: When I started to develop this penetrating movement, I realized that I could jam a head butt, a haymaker and so on. I started telling my students: "You're the spear tip. Just go right through the attacker." The SPEAR started as metaphor to get people to move toward danger because the paradox is that behaviorally, we move away from danger, while tactically, we need to move toward it.

BB: How do you position your arms when you implement the SPEAR?

Blauer: You hold your arms just outside 90 degrees so they form a triangle, which is one of the strongest geometric shapes. Your arms create a natural barrier between the attack and your most vulnerable areas—head, temples, ears, carotid region, brachial region, etc.

BB: Once someone learns the mental part of the SPEAR and the simple positioning of the arms, can all his previously learned martial arts techniques be blended with it?

Blauer: Yes. The SPEAR doesn't replace your system. Good information doesn't displace good information. Good information only displaces [crap]. The SPEAR allows you to get at what's good in your system. If you try to make your system work at what I call the "big-bang moment" of a real street fight, you may find yourself wondering what went wrong. The tactical flinch will intercept whatever he's doing and inflict some pain. The pain will cause doubt and hesitation on his part. That will give you a chance to engage him using the techniques from your style.

BB: When you use the SPEAR, are you trying to hurt the attacker or just stop him for a moment and negate his attack?

Blauer: If it is a real fight, you are trying to hurt the attacker. If you don't, the fight continues. Just remember that there is a moral and ethical distinction between hurting and injuring, and instructors must educate students on the legal considerations regarding self-defense. But the best part of the SPEAR system is that it's tactical and protective at the same time. If your attacker truly surprises you, you flinch, convert, make contact and defend. The serendipity of the SPEAR is that it often strikes at vulnerable points on the bad guy, and you weren't even going after them. The most important aspect of all this is that the SPEAR really doesn't interfere with your style. The SPEAR protects you in the moment of ambush—which is not addressed by most systems. The SPEAR allows you to get to your system and to hopefully escape safely. Think of it this way: The faster the attack, the faster the flinch, the sooner you can defend yourself. You can use your survival system to spontaneously protect yourself and use that natural flinch to accelerate your response.

STAND AND FIGHT:
Studying the Way MMA Fighters Scramble to Their Feet in the Cage Can Make You a Better Self-Defense Practitioner

by Stephan Kesting • Black Belt August 2009

WHEN THE MIXED MARTIAL ARTS hit North America on November 12, 1993—the day the Ultimate Fighting Championship debuted in Denver—competitors quickly learned that most fights wind up on the ground. For years, the prevailing wisdom had been that ground fighting is inevitable in most street altercations and that once the combatants go down, they're likely to stay there. When the majority of the fights that took place in the octagon followed that pattern, it was confirmed.

I've sparred with several professional MMA fighters over the years, and all of them were very difficult to keep down. They seemed to constantly mix conventional guard attacks such as sweeps and submissions with attempts to stand up. That made them unpredictable, and unpredictability is a quality that's tough to take on. Making things worse for their opponents is the fact that a fight that rapidly switches between stand-up and the ground can be very tiring for a person who hasn't honed his cardio to keep up with that sort of pace.

Lesson learned: Although most fights go to the ground, you don't have to stay there, and that applies as much to self-defense encounters as it does to sporting bouts. In that spirit, the following four stand-up techniques are presented. No matter which art you practice, they'll put you on the path to becoming a better martial artist.

THE SOLO STAND-UP

This move forms the foundation of most stand-up strategies. If this reality-based approach to fighting is relatively new to you, this is the place to start. The best part is that you can practice it on your own.

When you use the solo stand-up in real life, you'll want to do it quickly. In training, however, make sure that you start slowly and then gradually increase your speed. Running through it in slow motion ensures that your hands and feet are exactly where they need to be and that you're not simply relying on momentum to get up.

The key to doing this move correctly is to pendulum your body backward as your weight is supported on one hand and one foot. Dragging any part of your body on the ground will slow you down and increase your vulnerability.

SOLO STAND-UP: Stephan Kesting starts in a side breakfall position (1). He rises onto his elbow, keeping his other arm up to protect his face (2). He then sits upright, posting his hand behind him (3). He lifts his butt off the ground and kicks forward with his bottom leg (4), after which he retracts his kicking leg and swings it between his posted hand and foot (5). Finally, he stands and assumes a balanced fighting position (6).

Photos courtesy of Stephan Kesting

BASIC STAND-UP VS. AN OPPONENT

This technique is designed to function when your opponent is standing over you. You're keeping him at bay by bicycle-kicking his legs and body. Unfortunately, if you stop doing that so you can stand, you'll give him an opportunity to punch or kick you.

The solution entails doing three things in rapid succession: getting up, keeping at least one hand raised for protection and moving backward. This creates a demilitarized zone in which you're momentarily safe from his attacks. It's worth repeating that the success of this solution hinges on doing the steps as quickly as possible, almost simultaneously.

The moves you make are similar to those of the solo stand-up. The only difference is the addition of the leg kicks right before you swing your body backward and regain your footing.

BASIC STAND-UP VS. AN OPPONENT: Having been knocked down, Stephan Kesting must start fighting from his back (1). He keeps his eyes on his opponent as he rises onto his right elbow (2). He continues to come up, shielding his face with his left arm (3). Next, Kesting lifts his butt and shifts forward so he can reach his foe's knee with a kick (4). He immediately retracts his kicking leg and moves it under his body (5), then stands (6).

BRAZILIAN JIU-JITSU, SUBMISSION GRAPPLING AND MMA

Submission grappling has as its objective the scoring of points and/or the submission of the opponent. To accomplish that, practitioners use a variety of joint locks and chokes. They usually opt not to wear a *gi*, which increases the amount of speed and athleticism required to win while limiting the options for sweeping and submission techniques.

For the most part, submission grappling is based on Brazilian *jiu-jitsu*, a South American grappling art descended from pre-World War II judo, which in turn was heavily influenced by the classical *jujutsu* systems of medieval Japan. The influence of Brazilian jiu-jitsu on submission grappling can be seen in the positions and submissions commonly used in the sport.

Other arts have also left their mark on submission grappling. The most common takedowns come from freestyle wrestling. Numerous leg locks come from *sambo* and catch-as-catch-can wrestling, the ancestor of pro wrestling. Many top submission grapplers also compete in mixed-martial arts events, thus bringing a higher intensity level to the sport.

Techniquewise, submission grappling is similar to what's seen in the Ultimate Fighting Championship and similar events, minus the strikes and kicks. Positions and maneuvers that would be advantageous in a real fight—such as passing the guard and achieving the mount—are rewarded with points.

Training in submission grappling typically involves significant amounts of sparring, or "rolling." Bouts with a resisting opponent are considered crucial in the development of the skills and attributes needed for high-level performance.

—*S.K., Alexander Kask*

BUTTERFLY-GUARD STAND-UP

This defense begins from a different position, one that grapplers and MMA stylists call the butterfly guard. It refers to an orientation in which you're sitting with your feet positioned between your kneeling adversary's thighs. As such, your legs are your secret weapons because most untrained people don't know how they can be employed at such close range.

You control his arms to mitigate the threat, then lean forward for a bear hug. Once you've secured your hold on his torso, lean back and use your legs to lift. Immediately drop him on the ground and shove him away. Then swing one leg backward and get to your feet the way you learned in the solo stand-up. At that point, you can flee or counterattack.

Photos courtesy of Stephan Kesting

BUTTERFLY-GUARD STAND-UP: With his opponent in the butterfly guard, the martial artist defends against his strikes (1). He ducks his head and places it against the man's chest, securing a body lock with both arms (2). The defender hops his hips forward and elevates the opponent using his legs (3). He then drops him and kicks him away, stretching out his body (4). Using the space he's created, the defender pulls back his right leg (5) and stands, after which he drives a knee strike into the man's face (6).

HIP-BUMP STAND-UP FROM THE CLOSED GUARD

This self-defense strategy begins in the closed guard, a position that has you holding your opponent between your legs with your ankles crossed behind him. The position facilitates attacking and defending, but it makes standing up a little tricky because your foe can easily drop his weight on top of you.

To get to your feet from this position, you must use a technique known as the hip bump to create room. It involves lifting your hips and thrusting them forward, essentially using them as a battering ram to drive your opponent backward. Then, before he can settle his weight back down on your torso, swing one of your legs backward and stand up. It's a powerful technique that has been proved effective in MMA competition, but it requires attention to detail and lots of practice to be effective.

There are two keys to developing the four stand-up methods described earlier. The first is to build your knowledge of the techniques themselves. You need to learn what the correct steps are, where your hands and feet go, how to move your body, and so on.

The other key, at least for the second, third and fourth techniques, is to practice with an opponent who offers the right amount of resistance. Grab a partner, put him on top of you and tell him not to let you stand up—but caution him that offering too much opposition at the outset can stifle your ability to assimilate the movements. Once you're able to regularly get to your feet despite his best efforts to hold you down, you're well on your way to mastering these stand-up strategies.

If you're like most of your peers in the martial arts, you've worked long and hard to develop your hand and foot strikes. If you want them to remain your first line of defense, that's great. Continue to develop your skills. You don't have to become a grappler to be able to fight a grappler. Just make sure that you know how to get back to your feet should such an adversary take you to the ground. That way, you'll be able to use all those great punches and kicks in your arsenal.

HIP-BUMP STAND-UP FROM CLOSED GUARD: From inside Stephan Kesting's closed guard, the opponent throws punches (1). Kesting deflects them and sits up, reaching over the man's left shoulder and scooting his hips to the left (2). He then lifts his hips, bumping his adversary to the right (3). The bump creates enough room for Kesting to pull his right leg out (4). Exploiting the opening, Kesting can counterattack with a front head lock (5) or step back and disengage (6).

THE X-FACTOR:

How to Introduce Spontaneity and Unpredictability Into Your Reality-Based Self-Defense Training

by Ari Kandel • Black Belt July 2009

LIKE IT OR NOT, human beings are creatures of habit. We want to know what's going to happen and when it's going to start. In the *dojo,* we're most comfortable when we know precisely which kick our partner will throw and precisely how our *sensei* expects us to block and counter. Unfortunately, self-defense isn't quite so predictable, which is why we have to keep the X-factors always in mind.

1. We don't know when we'll be attacked. It can happen any day at any time. Or not. When it does happen, we don't know exactly when our ambusher will choose to punch or at what moment an "interview" conducted by an assailant-in-waiting will justify a pre-emptive strike.

2. We don't know where we'll be attacked. We don't know what the terrain will be or whether we'll be hit from behind, from the side, from above or from below. We may be standing, sitting or lying down.

3. We don't know who will attack us or how many of them will be involved. Few predators fit a profile. We may not even see the one who jumps us. If one shows himself before things get physical, we still won't really know whom we're dealing with. Drugs, psychosis and adrenaline can affect him in ways that aren't obvious until the fight is on. Multiple attackers won't stand in front of us; it's more common for one to try to distract us while others rush in to take us by surprise.

4. We don't know how they'll attack. Even the movements of our sparring partners are unpredictable. On the street, the addition of weapons—concealed or otherwise—makes things worse. Ambushes, distractions, thrown objects and the terrain also come into play.

5. We don't know the circumstances under which we'll be attacked. While some self-defense programs teach "likely" scenarios such as bar fights, carjackings and holdups, attacks can also happen in unexpected situations when we're least prepared to deal with them. While avoiding situations likely to lead to violence is advisable and effective in decreasing the odds of being attacked, it's not an absolute cure.

The most dangerous attacks usually begin at an unknown time and place, from an unknown angle, by an unknown person using unknown methods, in an unknown situation. Spontaneous adaptability is key to survival.

Obviously, as students of reality-based self-defense, we must learn how to spontaneously improvise tactics and movement that will help us deal with such variables. The abilities we develop must go far deeper than the ones that are cultivated in sparring matches and "unscripted" scenarios.

Unfortunately, it's virtually impossible to achieve complete spontaneity in martial arts training, insofar as we know going into a workout that we'll be required to deal with violence on some level. The only way around this would be for someone to "attack" us unexpectedly outside the dojo as we go about our lives. However, it's not possible to do that with any degree of realism while maintaining a reasonable level of safety and legality for all involved.

What is possible, however, is to maximize spontaneity within the limits of the training session. When we run through a drill or scenario, we must make sure that at least some of the specifics are unknown to us. The following are a few suggested methods, used by self-defense authority John Perkins in his Guided Chaos classes, for injecting some spontaneity into group training.

DRILL NO. 1

The student stands with his eyes closed and spins in a circle. At the command of "Go," he must open his eyes and attack a small target such as a focus mitt or HammerHead using a barrage of strikes, then run to a designated area. The instructor holding the target can position it anywhere around the student, at any angle or distance.

Variation A

While awaiting the verbal cue, the student gets smacked or pushed from any direction. He must instantly regain his balance and composure and counterattack. If the student is sufficiently trained, a "fright reaction" should occur.

Photo courtesy of Ari Kandel

In Group Drill No. 1 Variation B, the student must strike multiple targets that are moved into position while his eyes are closed.

Variation B

Multiple small targets are added while the student's eyes are closed. They can be moved independently and erratically. The student must hit all of them as quickly as possible, in any order. "Hit" and "No Hit" markings can be used on the targets to indicate which ones should be struck and which should be ignored.

Variation C

In a darkened room, strobe lights are turned on the instant the student opens his eyes.

Variation D

Kicking shields, focus mitts, a thick mat, plastic bottles, etc. are thrown around the student's feet just before he opens his eyes.

The body mechanics needed to hit the targets with explosive, full-body power, no matter what the angle or distance, require extensive prior training. In addition to developing that ability, this drill can expose potentially fatal deficiencies.

GROUP DRILL NO. 2 VARIATION A/B: Students A and B stand back-to-back with their eyes closed, awaiting a verbal cue (1). At that point, student B can be replaced by two different students or instructors (2). The "fight" can be initiated with a shove, after which student A will open his eyes and respond (3).

DRILL No. 2

Two students stand back-to-back, close but not touching. Their eyes are closed. On command, they turn toward each other and "fight" with an intensity appropriate to their skill level for about five seconds. On the command of "Break," they run to separate designated areas.

Variation A

While awaiting the verbal cue, one student gets pushed into the other, triggering the action.

Variation B

While awaiting the cue, one student gets replaced by two instructors or two larger students, both of whom face the other student. On the command of "Go," the unsuspecting student must deal with the stacked odds.

Variation C

While awaiting the cue, one student gets replaced by another student or instructor who grabs the first student in a chokehold or executes a clinch or takedown to initiate the action. If they fall, the student must fight to disengage and escape within five seconds.

Variation D

While awaiting the cue, one student gets replaced by three instructors holding striking shields or dummies. They proceed to surround and crush the first student to initiate the action.

Variation E

While awaiting the cue, one student is handed a training knife, padded stick or fake gun. He has the option to conceal it for later use, deploy it as soon as he hears the cue or use it before the cue is given. He may "hold up" the first student by grabbing him around the neck and yanking him off-balance while threatening him with the gun or knife or choking him with the stick.

These drills can go a long way toward improving a student's spontaneity for self-protection. They'll train him to have no preconceived notions about what can happen in a violent incident—to be prepared for everything by anticipating nothing. The first few times they're run, there's likely to be hesitation and confusion, which will usually spell doom for the student. He must clear his mind of anticipation and pattern seeking. He must learn to perceive and adapt to the situation while not being misguided by his expectations.

Spontaneity is relatively easy to practice in a group context because we have partners to provide unpredictable cues and manipulate the environment. Developing spontaneity on our own, however, is more difficult because any internally generated cue or decision is obviously predictable by us, but there are some methods for adding a little spontaneity to solo sessions.

Photo courtesy of Ari Kandel

The effectiveness of solo training can be enhanced by using specially designed playlists that work on most MP3 players. When started, they provide audio cues that initiate different self-defense responses.

SOLO DRILL NO. 1

Start a heavy bag swinging in a wide circle, then close your eyes, spin and jump into the area around which the bag is moving. The instant you detect the location of the bag—it may hit you or graze you, or you might feel the breeze as it swings by—open your eyes and attack the bag with maximum ferocity for about five seconds, then escape. Don't try to stop, control or push it. Move your body to penetrate it with maximum power at whatever angle and distance the bag dictates. Shift and sidestep—but don't back up—to avoid getting hit while you attack. If you can hang multiple bags in close proximity and get them all swinging at once, it's even better.

SOLO DRILL NO. 2

Get a technological edge. The Web site martialrealists.com offers free downloadable spontaneity-training tools. They're playlists of sound files for your MP3 player that you run in shuffle mode. The tracks consist of verbal commands with various time delays. When you use shuffle mode, you get audible cues with unpredictable timing. The first playlist gives the command "Hit" at random intervals, while the second uses the commands "Red" and "Black," which is based on a Guided Chaos drill that uses red and black targets.

At the simplest level, the Hit list can be used as follows: You face a heavy bag or other target. When the playlist starts, begin moving randomly. Spin in place, walk around the bag or perform the Guided Chaos exercise known as "polishing the sphere." On command, hit the bag quickly and powerfully from whatever position you happen to be in. No setting up, drawing back or readjustment before hitting is allowed. The better your balance, looseness, body unity and proprioception, the faster and harder you'll be able to strike. You can limit yourself to one striking tool—for example, palms or elbows—or hit with whatever is most efficient at the moment. Once the drill starts to flow, execute two hits per command and so on.

The Red and Black list permits you to add the element of multiple tasks and/or multiple targets. If you have two targets, Red can represent one and Black the other. Or Red can represent upper-body striking tools while Black represents kicks and knees. The intervals between the commands are generally longer than on the Hit list, enabling continuous attack or motion interrupted by spontaneous changes. Other playlists optimized for different types of training may become available, but even if all you have is the two described here, your ability to be spontaneous will grow immeasurably.

Editor's Note: Since the publication of this article, martialrealists.com no longer offers free downloadable playlists. However, the information is still relevant to martial artists who want to create their own training materials.

VIRTUAL REALITY:
Enhance Your Street Survivability with Tony Blauer's Cutting-Edge Self-Defense Drill!

by Dr. Eric Cobb • Black Belt May 2004

IT SEEMS THAT THESE DAYS, violence is on the rise, and prosecution of the good guys has reached an all-time high. As a savvy martial artist, you know the importance of learning a real-life street-survival curriculum that teaches more than just physical techniques. You realize that at some point in your training, you'll have to address the question of "appropriateness"—in other words, the belief that every encounter is different and may require protective skills that range from verbally defusing a potentially violent situation to terminating a threat in a life-or-death moment.

Tony Blauer, creator of the SPEAR system and president of Tactical Confrontation Management Systems, has developed a progressive set of drills to address that need. It's designed to instill confidence in students by teaching them the appropriateness of a variety of responses to any given assault. The drills constitute a major portion of his law-enforcement courses, and they're every bit as valuable for civilians interested in personal defense. Collectively called the Live Action Response Drill, they are among the most important training tools available to martial artists today.

EXTENUATING CIRCUMSTANCES

If you were to poll a group of martial arts students with a simple question—Is a two-handed shove a lethal-force attack?—most would quickly say it's not. Perhaps you're among them. But what if the shove takes place on the curb of a busy street or at the edge of a bridge? Can the recipient of such a push sustain a lethal injury? Of course.

Imagine this scenario: You answer a knock at your door in the early evening. As soon as your hand turns the knob, the door is shoved open, knocking you backward. You're then grabbed by the shirt and pushed against the wall. As you recover your senses, you think about how you can respond. Will you thrust your fingers into your attacker's eyes? Will you pull the knife from your pocket and begin slicing and dicing? Will you grab an improvised weapon from the table and slam it into his face?

Before you answer, consider one more bit of information: The "attacker" is your younger brother, who's just returned from boot camp. He's out to show you how tough he is now that he's made it through and earned his first leave. Now are any of the responses listed above or the ones that ran though your head when you first visualized this scenario appropriate? Probably not.

MORE THAN PHYSICAL

One of the greatest dangers of studying the martial arts is that you can wind up learning only physical responses for dealing with threats. It brings to mind an old saying: If all you've got is a hammer, everything begins to look like a nail. In martial arts speak: If you always train to respond to physical aggression with extreme violence, you're less likely to think about talking your way out. And that can leave you on shaky ground—legally, ethically and morally.

Review the scenario described above, but make the imaginary attacker a masked man with a bowie knife. How does that affect your mind-set and response? Other factors can further complicate your job. For example, how would you respond if you were home alone? What if your spouse and children were in the living room watching television? Each scenario dictates a different response. When you begin to view your training from this perspective, the need for creative drills that teach appropriateness becomes all the more apparent.

That's where the Live Action Response Drill comes in. It familiarizes you with four potentially appropriate responses to any given assault: verbal defuse, verbal defuse leading to stun-and-run tactics, verbal defuse leading to stun-and-control tactics, and verbal defuse leading to termination of the threat. The following is a brief examination of them and the ways they can apply to an attack.

PHYSICAL TRAINING: To be realistic, martial arts training must include plenty of practice of the physical techniques that will serve you best on the street. Here, Tony Blauer (left) faces an assailant (1). As the man initiates a roundhouse kick (2), Blauer slams a low kick into the assailant's supporting leg while making sure he protects his head (3).

VERBAL DEFUSE

A Tactical Confrontation Maximum System maxim holds that those who are willing to talk can usually be persuaded to walk. Put differently, if a potential attacker has not yet physically assaulted you, there's a good chance that appropriate verbal skills can de-escalate the tension and allow the involved parties to walk away unscathed.

Verbally defusing a situation is an art and science in and of itself, one that warrants extensive study of predator/prey psychology, choice speech patterns and other verbal tools. For the majority of martial artists, it's the most overlooked part of training.

VERBAL DEFUSE LEADING TO STUN-AND-RUN TACTICS

If you're unable to verbally defuse an assault, in many instances the wisest and safest course of action, from a physical and legal perspective, is to create enough distance and time to escape the threat. Stun-and-run tactics typically use quick, nontelegraphic strikes to disorient and psychologically unbalance the attacker long enough to enable you to flee. Again, this is something to which most martial artists devote insufficient time.

When you examine the concept that what you do in training is what you'll do in real life—only at a lower skill level—the need to practice the actual physical tactics of stun-and-run becomes evident. An example involves placing two chairs at one end of the *dojo* and designating the area between them as a safety zone. During practice, the defender is tasked with stunning the attacker, then running to safety. It's an incredibly beneficial drill, especially when incorporated into women's and children's self-defense classes.

Tony Blauer (left) teaches that those who are willing to talk can usually be persuaded to walk. It is the essence of his verbal-defuse tactic.

VERBAL DEFUSE LEADING TO STUN-AND-CONTROL TACTICS

In many instances, it becomes necessary not only to stun an attacker after verbal attempts have failed but also to control him until the authorities arrive or other help materializes. That's why the next section of Blauer's drill uses the actual physical tactics that come into play—usually a combination of nontelegraphic strikes and street-smart grappling moves.

When would stun-and-control be appropriate? Again, the scenario dictates everything. Perhaps you're a nightclub doorman who's forced to deal with a belligerent patron. Maybe the attacker is a drunken relative who is insisting on driving himself home and growing physically violent at your offers to be his designated driver. The only limitation to this part of the drill—and the application of its lesson—is your imagination.

Tony Blauer's stun-and-control tactic usually begins with a disorienting strike, then moves on to a grappling technique designed to hold the assailant until help arrives.

VERBAL DEFUSE LEADING TO TERMINATION OF THE THREAT

In stage four of the drill, ending the threat is the directive. The emphasis is now on employing your full close-quarters arsenal to debilitate the attacker as quickly as possible. Another TCMS maxim—real fights happen in the space of a phone booth—can help you overcome any challenges you may encounter here. For best results, concentrate on developing your proficiency at executing elbow strikes, knee thrusts, head butts, eye gouges, pinches and bites.

BACK TO THE BEGINNING

Now return to the original scenario and visualize a situation involving the same attack. You can choose any one of the four responses taught in the Live Action Response Drill. It changes things, doesn't it?

You should be able to apply this knowledge to all types of potentially dangerous encounters. You'll find that your decision-making skills have improved dramatically and your physical tactics have become more refined. In short, you're better prepared to handle violence while minimizing the legal and moral entanglements that often follow the use of force.

WINNING ALL THE BATTLES

Whenever Tony Blauer instructs new students, he points out an often-overlooked fact: Real-world confrontations require a toolbox that's different from the one you use in the *dojo* or the ring.

While traditional training methods, drills and sparring exercises can improve your conditioning, flexibility, speed, strength and tool development, they rarely instill the moral, legal and ethical platforms necessary to survive on the streets today.

To drive home that point, Blauer created a principle called the Three Fights. A favorite among progressive law-enforcement trainers, it states that in any fight, there are actually three separate battles:

- you vs. you (requiring fear management, correct mind-set, etc.)
- you vs. your opponent (requiring realistic personal-defense skills)
- you vs. the legal system (requiring an understanding of self-defense law)

Each battle demands a different set of skills and tactics, and the Live Action Response Drill is among the most useful tools for developing your capabilities to function in each one. When performed with intensity and focus, it will teach you much about yourself, your ability to control your fear and your capacity for dealing with the emotional and psychological stress that is sure to follow.

It also offers a safe and effective method for pressure-testing your tools and tactics against an opponent, and that's a vital step in developing real-world efficacy. Perhaps most important, it provides a foundation of appropriate responses to different threats, which will empower you to articulate how and why you acted the way you did to protect yourself.

—E.C.

GROUND SURVIVAL:
Essential Component of Reality-Based Personal Protection

by Jim Wagner • Black Belt April 2006

IN MOST CONFLICT SITUATIONS, the ground is the last place you want to be. You can end up on the ground because a suspect forces you there (a takedown) or because you inadvertently trip and fall. Either way, once committed to terra firma, you're forced to give up several key tactical advantages that you'd normally have in a standing position: mobility, retreat and escape options, long-range striking capabilities and most offensive positioning.

On the other hand, there are times when going to the ground can be your best choice for survival, such as in a firearms or grenade attack. These are instances in which you should hit the deck as quickly as you can and seek cover. The advantages to being on the ground in such situations include maintaining a reduced target profile, projecting a nonthreatening posture, and finding low-level cover and concealment.

Because many conflicts do end up going to the ground, whether intentionally or unintentionally, it's an important component of Reality-Based Personal Protection.

Unfortunately, much of what's being taught as "ground fighting" in martial arts schools is actually sport-based. Like many systems whose origins are in the military arts (the term "martial arts" literally means "war arts"), they've evolved into a sport or follow sportlike rules. Although there are many similarities between sport-based martial arts and Reality-Based Personal Protection, sport-based arts lack the additional tactics that make them effective in actual survival situations.

Establishing a ground-survival program entails more than just taking your current ground-fighting training and "going harder" or adding a few punches or kicks to your existing skills. It involves using elements that make the training truly reality-based. The following nine elements will help you reach this goal.

MAT TRAINING

Although in a real-life situation you'll probably fight on hard ground, you still need to train on mats or other soft surfaces for safety. However, instead of always laying the mats out flat, build a plywood slope or put items under them (such as kicking shields, boxing gloves, etc.) to make a bumpy, uneven surface. You can also cover them with sand, party ice or other clean debris (clean, empty plastic bottles, newspapers, used clothes, etc.).

By adding "garnish" to your mats, you provide a greater degree of realism, thus conditioning yourself to fight on "contaminated surfaces."

TRAINING IN DARKNESS

Military special-operations personnel and cops always train in low-light scenarios. You should do the same because most violent crimes occur during the hours of darkness.

When practicing your ground-survival techniques, try turning out the lights from time to time or

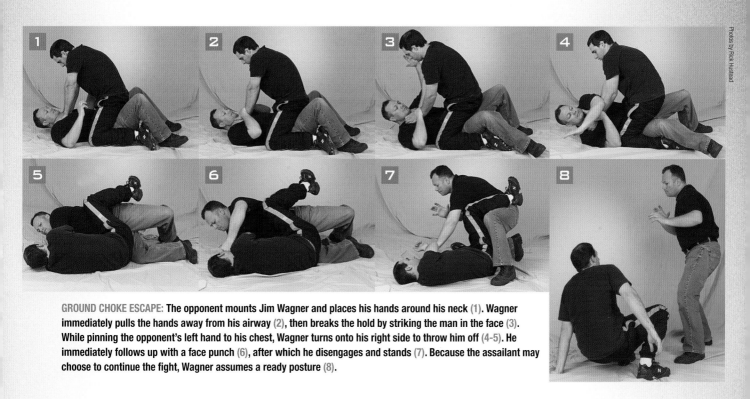

Photos by Rick Hustead

GROUND CHOKE ESCAPE: The opponent mounts Jim Wagner and places his hands around his neck (1). Wagner immediately pulls the hands away from his airway (2), then breaks the hold by striking the man in the face (3). While pinning the opponent's left hand to his chest, Wagner turns onto his right side to throw him off (4-5). He immediately follows up with a face punch (6), after which he disengages and stands (7). Because the assailant may choose to continue the fight, Wagner assumes a ready posture (8).

dimming them. This will simulate a dark alley, bar, nightclub or even your home in the middle of the night.

REALISTIC APPAREL

Wear what you'll fight in. If you're a cop, security guard, soldier, ambulance driver or another type of professional who's subject to altercations, practice your ground fighting in full gear: ballistic vest, gun belt, boots, etc. If you're a civilian living in a cold climate, try your techniques while wearing a winter coat, gloves and hat. If you train only in comfortable workout clothes, you could be handicapped when a real situation arises.

By wearing the clothes you'll most likely wear during a physical conflict, you'll quickly discover what part of your gear permits or restricts movement. The goal is to find out these things in training rather than in an actual conflict.

GROUND TRAINING

Practicing strikes from the ground is just as important as learning them from a standing position. Most good rape-prevention courses start by having the students practice how to fight from the ground. Why? Because the ground (a bed, car seat, floor) is where the victim will likely end up in a sexual assault. So why not start from the place where most of the fighting is done?

Learn to strike from your back and sides. Use boxing gloves, kicking shields and other gear and devices. The key to striking from the ground is to rotate or torque your body into each blow.

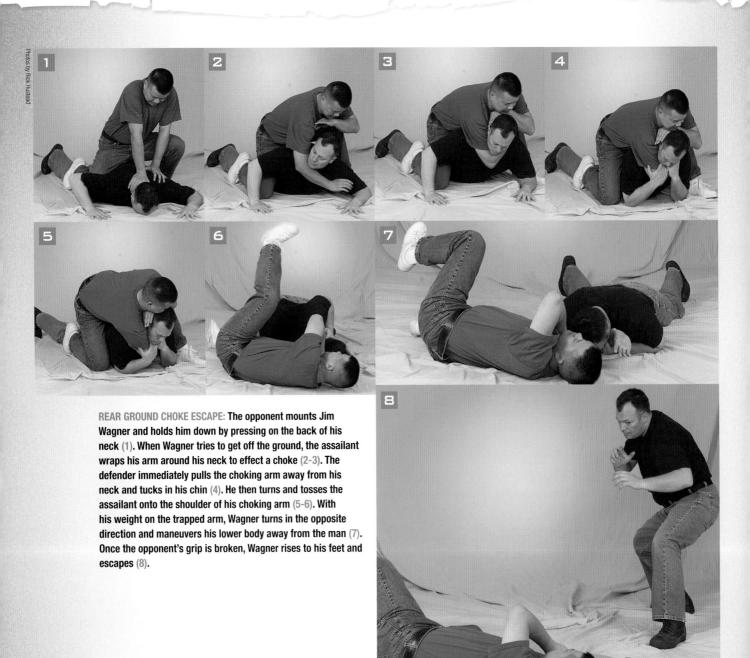

REAR GROUND CHOKE ESCAPE: The opponent mounts Jim Wagner and holds him down by pressing on the back of his neck (1). When Wagner tries to get off the ground, the assailant wraps his arm around his neck to effect a choke (2-3). The defender immediately pulls the choking arm away from his neck and tucks in his chin (4). He then turns and tosses the assailant onto the shoulder of his choking arm (5-6). With his weight on the trapped arm, Wagner turns in the opposite direction and maneuvers his lower body away from the man (7). Once the opponent's grip is broken, Wagner rises to his feet and escapes (8).

EXPAND YOUR STRIKING REPERTOIRE

Incorporate arm, leg and head strikes into your conflict rehearsals. Whenever your training is on the ground, don't limit your striking techniques. Obviously, contact should be light to medium, but it needs to be done to promote muscle memory.

Safety gear can be worn to protect the "attacker" when you practice eye gouges, throat grabs, groin squeezes and other moves.

TRAINING WEAPONS

Incorporate the use of rubber, plastic or foam weapons into your scenarios. Start on the ground with your hands and your partner's hands on the same weapon, such as a training gun or knife. Upon hearing a "Go!" command, you and he struggle for the weapon. The one who gains control of it can use it against his opponent.

Other situations can begin with wrestling, then the "attacker" can pull out a concealed rubber knife and use it in the middle of the fight. Such realistic training teaches you to keep your eyes open at all times so you can immediately deal with whatever crops up.

ATTACKERS UNDER THE INFLUENCE

How do you simulate training with a person who's high on drugs or violent from ingesting alcohol? Simple. Make sure the "attacker" is fresh and rested before a match, while you do calisthenics or run until you're exhausted. Then return to the mat to grapple with your energized opponent. This simulates the edge a person will have when he's under the influence—especially of hallucinogens. It's this kind of drill that may save your life one day because you'll be able to go the extra distance even when you feel you have no more strength left.

Keep in mind, however, that attackers and opponents under the influence of alcohol and other substances—particularly stimulants (cocaine and crystal methamphetamine) or hallucinogens (LSD, PCP and to a lesser extent, Ecstasy)—can be volatile and unpredictable. Their perception of reality, pain and consequences can be severely altered so as to negate the effects of your defensive tactics. For example, PCP users often feel no pain and have been known to emerge from usage episodes bloodied and injured from unknowingly falling, walking through glass, etc. Such opponents bring an elevated danger to the situation and should never be underestimated.

MULTIPLE ATTACKERS

The possibility of being attacked by multiple assailants while you're on the ground is scary, but you have to train for it. One of the best ways to prepare begins with the "victim" putting on a helmet to give the attackers the option of kicking to the head (using light contact only). One attacker will typically hold the victim while the other kicks or punches him. (Gang members tend to use this tactic because they hunt in packs.)

The key to survival is using fast and effective techniques and getting to your feet as soon as possible. In real fights, you can't afford to roll around on the ground doing fancy blocks and strikes.

INJURY SIMULATION

It's possible to get injured in a real fight, so it's crucial to simulate getting injured in training so you can learn how to press on despite the pain. Here's a crude but effective method: While you and your opponent are grappling, your instructor unexpectedly pours a bucket of ice water on you. The sudden shock simulates the feeling you would experience when wounded: Your breathing becomes rapid and shallow, your clothes get wet (from blood and sweat) and your muscles tense up.

A more intense drill involves having your instructor shoot you and your partner with an AirSoft gun. You must wear goggles to protect your eyes, but the rest of your body should be covered by only a T-shirt and workout pants. The instructor then takes aim from across the room and shoots each of you once on a limb. The sting of the plastic projectile's impact simulates the pain associated with a stab wound or a gunshot wound. The shock may make you writhe in pain, but soon you'll learn to override your natural instincts and continue the fight until you're victorious or able to escape.

Breath control and mental focus are the keys to overcoming the pain you'll experience in these exercises. Together, they'll help you develop the will to survive, which can be the most valuable attribute in your arsenal for the street.

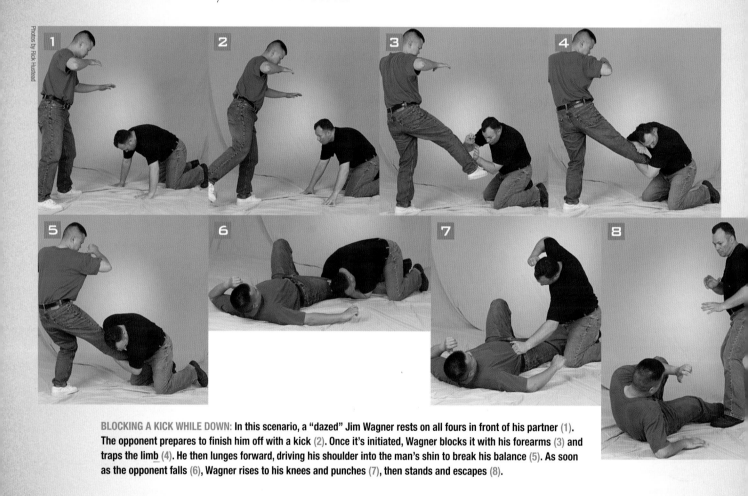

Photos by Rick Hustead

BLOCKING A KICK WHILE DOWN: In this scenario, a "dazed" Jim Wagner rests on all fours in front of his partner (1). The opponent prepares to finish him off with a kick (2). Once it's initiated, Wagner blocks it with his forearms (3) and traps the limb (4). He then lunges forward, driving his shoulder into the man's shin to break his balance (5). As soon as the opponent falls (6), Wagner rises to his knees and punches (7), then stands and escapes (8).

DISTRACT, DISABLE AND DESTROY:
Combat Hapkido's Low-Line Kicking
Guarantees Supremacy on the Street!

by Floyd Burk • Black Belt March 2004

"THE BIGGEST ADVANTAGE attackers have over their victims is the element of surprise," claims combat-*hapkido* master John Pellegrini. "Attackers expect their targets to freeze up, allowing them to gain immediate psychological and physical superiority."

Those are sobering words, to be sure, but if nothing else, they should inspire you to do everything in your power to bolster your defenses and incorporate the element of surprise into your planned responses to attack. One of the best ways to do that is to arm yourself with combat hapkido's low-line kicking methods, which mesh with any number of joint locks and follow-up strikes for a cool combination of controlled fury.

GOOD BEGINNING

Pellegrini advocates employing low-line kicks as a first line of defense to surprise your opponent, then distract and disable him, thus making it easier for you to destroy him with a follow-up. Such kicks are just one of the components that distinguish combat hapkido from other Korean fighting systems. Instead of the customary jumping and spinning techniques, you need to focus on kicks that lash out at waist level or lower, he says.

Low-line kicks are ideal for street fighting, mostly because it's fairly easy to avoid telegraphing your intentions when doing them. Other key advantages include the ability to generate maximum power, the maintenance of better balance (because your center of gravity stays lower), the ability to ruin your opponent's mobility (by hammering his leg muscles), and the option of attacking his groin and certain parts of his legs to shock his nervous system and buckle his body.

When combined with combat hapkido's awareness position, which the art uses instead of traditional stances, the aforementioned advantages can give you the upper hand and make it easier for you to execute a finishing throw, joint lock or hand strike, Pellegrini says.

FIGHTING COMBO NO. 1

An ego-pumped punk says he's going to pound you into the ground. He lunges at you with a head punch—then finds himself flat on his back with one of your knees on his head and the other against his spine. To top it off, his arm feels as if it's twisted like a pretzel.

The combat-hapkido solution begins with you facing your attacker with your left foot forward and your forearms horizontal at chest level. Your hands are open and ready for action. As he closes the gap and initiates the right-hand strike, step forward and to the outside with your left leg. Simultaneously use your right hand to parry his punch, then grab his wrist. The path is now open to disable him with a roundhouse kick to his right leg.

Next, use your left hand to seize the elbow of the arm you just grabbed. Lift the limb, then circle it downward while you pivot counterclockwise. That will cause him to fall on his left side. Once he does, drop your left knee onto the side of his head and dig your other knee into his lower back while maintaining control of his arm. Complete the immobilization by cranking his wrist. Increase the pressure as needed.

"Martial artists train with other martial artists who are constantly being polite to one another, bowing, helping each other up and that kind of thing," Pellegrini says. "While this can be a lot of fun, it's more likely that a lunatic lacking in morals is going to be who you're defending against. Consequently, you need to do role-playing where you and various partners take turns assuming the role of the lunatic. Be creative but stay realistic. That way, you'll be mentally prepared for this type of attack, and surprise and fear won't beat you."

Photos by Rick Hustead

AGAINST A PUNCH: John Pellegrini (left) assumes the combat-*hapkido* awareness position in front of his assailant (1). When the attacker punches, Pellegrini evades the blow and traps the arm (2), then slams a roundhouse kick into his leg (3). He grasps the attacker's arm (4) and executes a spinning takedown (5). Once the attacker hits the ground, Pellegrini immobilizes him with his knees (6) and effects a wrist lock (7).

FIGHTING COMBO NO. 2

A hooligan threatens you, then grabs your arm in an effort to shock you into giving in to his demands. Your foot lashes out in a flash, leaving him with a ruptured groin and, after you fling him to the pavement, a bad case of road rash.

Begin in an awareness position that has your right foot forward. For the drill, your attacker assumes a left-side forward stance before grabbing your right wrist with his right hand. Direct a front snap kick into his groin. The force of the blow will cause him to double over.

You now have the opening you need to reverse his grip and put him into a two-handed wrist-flex (one hand holds his wrist and the other bends his fingers forward). Pull him toward you and lift your right elbow to smash him in the nose. Increase the tension of the wrist-flex and pivot about 20 degrees counterclockwise to throw him to the ground. Drop your left knee onto the side of his head and reposition your hands for a standing armbar that uses your upper leg as a fulcrum. He'll be as helpless as a baby.

Wise words from Pellegrini: "Whether you are a strong young person or a cagey 60-year-old, don't overestimate or underestimate your opponent. By hitting vulnerable targets and vital areas, you can do much damage to an unsuspecting combatant. Even if your physical gifts are limited, you should come out on top."

Photos by Rick Hustead

AGAINST A GRAB: When the attacker (left) grabs John Pellegrini's wrist (1), he responds with a snap kick to the groin (2). He then executes a two-handed wrist-flex (3) and an elbow smash to the face (4). To finish, he leverages him to the ground (5) and hyperextends the attackers arm (6).

FIGHTING COMBO No. 3

Things are getting ugly fast. Joe Schmo reaches for your throat with the ultimate goal of relieving you of your life, but your quick-kick counterattack and whirling takedown leave him writhing in pain and begging for mercy.

Your self-defense training should prepare you to act instinctively whenever an opponent goes for your neck. That's why the combat-hapkido response to the scenario described above involves immediately grabbing the attacking hand with your right hand. Yank it down just enough to clear your windpipe, then slam an angled kick into the quadriceps of his lead leg. Wrap your left arm around his trapped limb so you can free your right hand, which is used to launch a tiger-mouth strike at his throat. Your same-side elbow then smashes into his solar plexus.

Continue your defense with a counterclockwise spinning takedown that lands him flat on his back. Maintain your hold on his Adam's apple. Finish him with a knee to the neck and an elbow/shoulder dislocation.

"The logical thing to do is protect your windpipe," Pellegrini advises. "Most other courses of action

Photos by Rick Hustead

AGAINST A CHOKE: The attacker reaches for John Pellegrini's neck, but Pellegrini intercepts the hand and keeps it away from his airway (1). He then drives an angled kick into the closest leg (2), entangles the choking arm (3) and shoots a tiger-mouth strike into the throat (4). Pellegrini follows up with an elbow strike to the solar plexus (5) and a takedown, after which he executes an arm lock and a choke (6).

RESPONDING TO THE CRITICS

If an award were given for stirring up controversy, combat-*hapkido* creator John Pellegrini would be the world champion of 2003. His opening statement in the cover story of the June 2003 issue of *Black Belt*—"Forget the fancy high kicks, lose the forms and stop wasting time with healing, meditation and breathing exercises or outdated weapons training"—was nearly as bold as the late Bruce Lee's infamous 1966 declaration that "all fixed set patterns are incapable of adaptability or pliability—the truth is outside of all fixed patterns."

While Pellegrini's views have incited many mainstream practitioners, most people respect him for his honesty and for the courage to make his claims publicly. And he hasn't backed down from his position. "The reason people [started] training in martial arts was to defend against brutal and barbaric enemies, but in the past few decades, the arts in general have become playground stuff," he says. "Winning trophies at tournaments, becoming proficient with ancient weapons [you'll] never be attacked with, and doing dance and gymnastics moves is not going to save your life.

"The pendulum is now swinging back to the other extreme. People are taking their self-defense training more seriously. They realize that at any moment, they may be confronted by terrorists or criminals and have to take action. People don't have years and years to stretch, learn forms and practice meditation while figuring out the existence of mankind. They need to be able to use their training immediately. Thus, instructors and students ought to use most of their class time to perfect the self-defense material, then do the fitness and health stuff on their own."

—*F.B.*

can leave you incapacitated. Since you never know what's coming, it's best to use what warriors call *mushin,* or the 'mind of no mind.' Don't form in your mind [an image of] what's going to happen. Instead, keep it clear so you can react and adapt without hesitation."

FIGHTING COMBO NO. 4

An enraged gangbanger is intent on cracking your skull with a club. You react instantaneously, making quick work of him with a wrist torque and a boot to the gut. In seconds, he's reduced to a quivering pile of jelly.

Assume the awareness position in front of your partner. When he swings his training weapon at your head, deflect it as you lean slightly to your left. Use your right hand to seize the hand he's using to hold the club, then twist it and the weapon in a semicircle until he can no longer control it. Follow up with a low-line kick to the body, which stuns him long enough for you to slap on a short-duration wrist lock and effect a disarm.

Technical tips: "When defending against a weapon at close quarters, remember that different ones require different disarming techniques. For bladed weapons, never grab the blade. Grab the hand holding the weapon, then take care of the opponent and the weapon. For gun disarms, seize the gun before executing the takedown or takeaway. There's more leeway when it comes to impact weapons, but I prefer to evade and get inside its trajectory, then clamp onto the limb holding the weapon. Then I take it away."

AGAINST A CLUB: John Pellegrini faces an armed attacker (1). The man swings his weapon, and Pellegrini evades the blow while he deflects and traps the attacker's arm (2). He then twists the limb (3) and sends a front kick into the man's torso (4). While the aggressor is stunned, Pellegrini applies pressure against the wrist (5) and completes the disarm (6).

SIGNS OF SUCCESS

With down-to-earth techniques such as the four described here, it's no wonder combat hapkido and its creator are enjoying unrivaled success in the martial arts community. Pellegrini reports rising sales of his videos and DVDs, as well as a one-year backlog in seminar and training camp appearances. Membership in his organization, the International Combat Hapkido Federation, has climbed to 250 schools located in more than 20 countries.

The reason for that success can be traced directly back to Pellegrini's efforts to distill his knowledge of the traditional arts down to its most functional essence, then pass it on to any martial artist who shows an interest. The formula certainly seems to be working.

Editor's Note: Since the publication of this article, John Pelligrini wrote his first book, *Combat Hapkido: The Martial Art for the Modern Warrior.*

COMBAT IN THE REAL WORLD:
Self-Defense Secrets From Security Expert Kelly McCann
Part 1
Interview by Robert W. Young • Black Belt June 2008

KELLY McCANN IS ONE OF THE MOST experienced real-world fighters you're likely to encounter. Scratch that. If you're not part of the military special-ops community or certain other government agencies, chances are slim that you'll ever meet him, let alone pick his brain for fighting secrets since he doesn't train the public. Fortunately, you can benefit from his knowledge and experience because *Black Belt* managed to hook up with the combatives expert during a recent trip he made to California.

Black Belt: What's your opinion of the material that's being taught in the civilian self-defense community?

Kelly McCann: I really don't have much to do with the civilian self-defense community, but it seems that there are far more "armchair" instructors than there are instructors who have a personal relationship with real violence. That's apparent from some of the DVDs and videos I've seen. The techniques are way too segmented, way too defensively focused—pretty impractical.

There are two problems with that. One, the armchair instructor doesn't understand how the body dysfunctions in a potentially lethal encounter or what you can expect your body to reasonably be able to do. Two, it means students who pursue self-defense from an armchair instructor often don't understand that there's not a painless way to learn because you have to be put under duress in training to do it.

You have to have a technique done to you in order to feel the effectiveness, and you have to do it to others to see that you can achieve an acceptable result. There are, of course, a lot of well-intentioned teachers; they simply lack experience with violence. There are also a lot of students who see training as more of a social event.

BB: To overcome that obstacle, must a student of self-defense seek out a teacher who has firsthand experience with violence, or is it sufficient to study under a teacher who's studied under someone who's experienced it?

McCann: You can learn from someone who's been properly trained but who doesn't have firsthand experience. It's critical that your instructor understands what the physiological effects of imminent danger are and how those effects diminish response ability, as well as how street violence occurs. The problem is, in the martial arts, a student usually has a subordinate position with respect to his instructor, and the student should never question the instructor. You can't ask, "Who are you and why should I listen to you?" Unfortunately, there are a lot of charlatans who can look the part to a newbie.

The second part of the solution is for the student to personally embark on a journey to understand what real violence is, how quickly it happens and under what conditions— including how a human being reacts under duress. There's a ton of literature about what you can and can't do when you suffer tunnel vision, auditory exclusion and physical dysfunctions.

After that, the student needs to find an instructor who will put him in those positions in training so he has to defend himself under duress—using sensory overloading, stressors, etc. Then the student will learn whether he really needs a right-hand technique, a left-hand technique and a two-hand technique—or just one technique that handles all those variables, which is what we believe. Choice reaction time should be minimized to increase the likelihood of success on the street.

BB: What aspect of civilian self-defense needs more emphasis?

McCann: You need to learn equally about when you'll be expected to fight and how you'll be expected to fight. You might be able to do a certain technique every time in a safe environment—and then completely fail on the street in an unfamiliar environment [because you're] under duress and in a compressed time cycle.

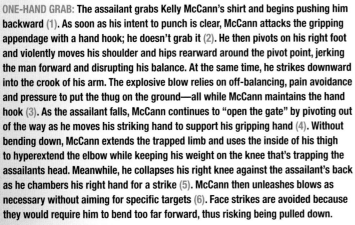

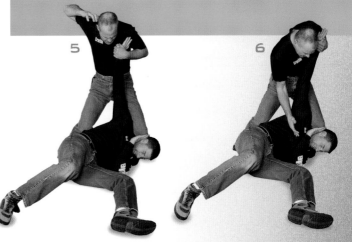

Photos by Thomas Sanders

ONE-HAND GRAB: The assailant grabs Kelly McCann's shirt and begins pushing him backward (1). As soon as his intent to punch is clear, McCann attacks the gripping appendage with a hand hook; he doesn't grab it (2). He then pivots on his right foot and violently moves his shoulder and hips rearward around the pivot point, jerking the man forward and disrupting his balance. At the same time, he strikes downward into the crook of his arm. The explosive blow relies on off-balancing, pain avoidance and pressure to put the thug on the ground—all while McCann maintains the hand hook (3). As the assailant falls, McCann continues to "open the gate" by pivoting out of the way as he moves his striking hand to support his gripping hand (4). Without bending down, McCann extends the trapped limb and uses the inside of his thigh to hyperextend the elbow while keeping his weight on the knee that's trapping the assailants head. Meanwhile, he collapses his right knee against the assailant's back as he chambers his right hand for a strike (5). McCann then unleashes blows as necessary without aiming for specific targets (6). Face strikes are avoided because they would require him to bend too far forward, thus risking being pulled down.

BB: Is too much time spent on empty-hand self-defense and not enough on weapons defense?

McCann: There's a liability issue related to that choice for instructors who deal routinely with the public, and rightfully so. In our litigious society, people might be able to come back on an instructor who reasonably and accurately taught techniques before putting the responsibility on the student to perfect those techniques and judge when to use them. A guy learns how to take away a weapon on Thursday and then tries to do it on Sunday outside a restaurant during a street robbery and gets shot. Now he's crippled. He's suing his instructor. That's not a concern for the students we train because they know they're far more likely to face those eventualities and have accepted the inherent risks involved in their jobs. It behooves them to get proficient at weapons techniques.

BB: Is that why military instructors readily teach soldiers how to disarm a gunman, while most civilian instructors say, "Just give him your wallet"?

McCann: Yes, and by the way, you should give him your wallet. If the soldier is on leave and confronted by [an armed assailant who wants] his wallet, he should give it up, too! Your wallet, your watch—no material possession is worth dying for. The problem is when the potentially violent encounter becomes about something else and your life is in danger. In our clients' world of work, the situations in which they would disarm someone have nothing to do with a robbery and everything to do with duty responsibility; that responsibility doesn't [apply] to the public.

BB: What kind of weapons should martial artists carry for self-defense, and what should they have at home?

McCann: The legal ones. Make sure you meet all your state's legal requirements before getting or carrying a weapon. OC gas (pepper spray) is great to carry because it's a distance weapon. You can use it early in an altercation, before you even make contact with the assailant, and not a lot of technique is required. When it's legal, an expandable baton is also great because it gives you distance. It's basically a stick, and everybody can use a stick with some degree of success.

BB: In states where the expandable baton is illegal, like California, is there a legal option that's just as good?

McCann: The pocket stick—also known as the *yawara* or *kubotan*—is good if you have the skills to use it, but it's not quite as effective as the expandable baton because you have to close with your attacker. Knives are certainly good—if you've got the guts to use one. A sharp instrument is a great weapon; trouble is, its use is generally viewed as felonious. If you ever use a knife in self-defense, you'll probably get killed in court. The opposing attorneys will undoubtedly say a higher standard applies because you've been trained and that you should have tried to ... blah, blah, blah. That's why OC gas and pocket sticks are better weapons for those who know how to use them.

BB: What about in the home? Are guns the answer?

McCann: Yes, and dogs. At home, you want layered security. You want to affect the thinking—the decision-making process and victim selection—of anyone who may be looking at breaking in. You want to make him think you're a hard target. For the first layer, you should have good lights around your house and good locks. If someone breaks in, the second layer is a dog. For the third layer, OC gas and maybe a gun—with the caveat that you have to be properly trained in combative shooting while under duress. A gun is good only if you'll use it and know when to use it. You also need to consider who else is in the home, who has access to the gun, and what safety measures need to be in place to protect it from theft and/or unauthorized use by a child.

The thing with guns is, a person may be a good shot, but that doesn't matter if he second-guesses himself right up to the last minute and doesn't shoot until it's too late. For that kind of person, OC gas is a better option.

Photos by Thomas Sanders

IMPACT WEAPON: Kelly McCann (left) faces Jack Stradley in the guard position (1). Because a bludgeon becomes increasingly dangerous as you move away from it, McCann opts to vault inside the arc of the weapon so he can neutralize it without having to control it (2). Attacking with his whole body, McCann indexes his right hand on the back of his head, resulting in a spearing elbow that's driven into the man's sternum or any nearby body part. The spearing elbow transitions into an ax hand that "hacks" the head/neck/face without being pulled back to chamber. McCann's left arm drops to the outside of the weapon arm and locks onto it by gripping it above the elbow. Next, the right hand hooks the man's neck (3) and yanks him down into a rising knee strike (4). McCann fixes his eyes on the body part that his final strike will hit: the back of the man's head/neck. As his foot drops to the ground, he pivots to generate power with his whole body, culminating in a slashing elbow to the back of the attacker's head (5). He finishes by stomping on a joint—preferably the elbow, knee or ankle—to immobilize the assailant (6).

BB: What's the value of improvised weapons? How can a person train to use them?

McCann: An improvised weapon is a mentality, not a tool. In other words, if you have the improvisational mentality, it doesn't matter what's at hand. You can use a pen to stab. You can fold a credit card and use it to cut a guy's face. You can grab a soda can and rip it in half—and you'll have two knives. Even a videocassette, slung into a guy's throat, can be more effective, and quicker, than an empty-hand technique.

BB: How do you teach that mentality?

McCann: You show your students how it's done by using a lot of examples, after which you teach the principles: how to create leverage, how to inflict pain, how to cut, how to see the "weapon" attributes in ordinary things.

BB: What are the best martial arts for students interested in reality-based self-defense?

McCann: The Philippine arts are one of the best choices because they're just so dirty—in a good

5 ESSENTIAL STRIKES
FOR REALITY-BASED SELF-DEFENSE

- *Hammerfist:* It's powerful, it's a gross-motor movement and you can quickly fire off one shot after another.

- *Face Mash:* Using your palm to hit your opponent in the face while you throw your body weight into it is very effective. If he can't see you, he can't hurt you. The goal is to hit him in the face and slam his head back. As his head moves backward, you'll likely have one or two fingers impact an eye.

- *Ax Hand:* It's another gross-motor movement. It's a little more involved because you have to know how to hit and how to chamber. You make the impact with any part of your arm from your elbow to the tip of your little finger. It's a linear technique, so you're intersecting your target, not trying to hit it like you do with a punch. That increases your chance of success.

- *Shin Kick:* In combatives, this has a different meaning than it does in Thai boxing. For us, a shin kick uses the instep of the boot to hit the guy's shin. The effect can be overwhelming. The Thai kick that uses the shin to strike the nerve in the thigh is great, but a lot of people can't articulate their hips enough to get the angle and power. You have to come outside, then downward and across as you step across in order to drag your weight through. You can't just snap the kick out.

- *Spearing Elbow:* The forward elbow strike is very effective. Any elbow strike is, actually.

Note that I left out the chin jab. The problem is, it's so potentially damaging that if it becomes something you rely on, you'll eventually hurt someone terribly.

—*Kelly McCann*

way—and utilitarian, and they're great for developing hand speed. When it comes to striking, *krav maga* has come a long way. It used to be just bad *jujutsu*—if you look at the book *Fighting Fit* by Col. David Ben-Asher of the Israeli Defense Force, you can see that—but it's evolved into a very good striking system.

BB: Did krav maga evolve here or in Israel?

McCann: It evolved here. It's remarkable. I was a krav maga member in the early '80s because I wanted to see what it was about. I wasn't that impressed. Now it's a fierce striking art. I also like some of the karate styles that are short on philosophy and religion and long on strength, power and short, linear movements. Same with some of the Korean styles that focus on power strikes. Actually, any martial art that's boiled down to its essentials will do. Unfortunately, instructors feel compelled to make their students think their particular style or "way" is best—all of it—but the truth is that if you boil down any style, you'll have very similar techniques that really work.

BB: Do the styles that are generally considered most applicable to the mixed martial arts—*muay Thai*, boxing and Brazilian *jiu-jitsu*—also work for reality-based self-defense?

McCann: Thai boxing is fantastic because it teaches knees, elbows and all that good stuff. Jiu-jitsu is super for conditioning, fosters a good, tough mentality and teaches you how to roll. Boxing is good for hand speed and hand techniques—a straight jab is still one of the toughest things to counter.

The departure is that we teach combatives only as a means to get to a weapon. On the street in Bosnia, Somalia, Kosovo or Baghdad against a huge guy who could pound my head flat, would I try to take him down and use a martial arts technique? No, if he meant to kill me, or in my judgment could or might kill me, I'd use my empty-hand skills to hold him off until I could get to my knife. He might take me down and try to hit me, but my right hand is going to be pulling that knife out of my pocket, and if I have to, I'm going to gut him like a fish to save my life. That's the difference: The goal in combatives isn't to use a technique; it's to win.

Of course, you need the moral authority to use that much physical force, and that comes from being avoidant. As a nonduty-bound civilian, you should fight only when you have no other choice. You have to lawfully adhere to the force continuum and can use the upper end of the force continuum—extreme force—only when you believe your life is in jeopardy.

BB: In the firearms community, it's often said that you should use your handgun to get to your rifle. Is it like that with respect to using your empty-hand skills to get to your weapon?

McCann: Absolutely. That's the role of combatives as we teach them. Getting to your weapon may not be the only thing you do once you have control of a situation, but you do want some type of weapon in your hand—whether it's OC gas or whatever. It just makes sense to have something that gives you an advantage.

There's no equality in a fight. In Iraq, there was an incident during the initial invasion in which a tank commander believed he saw the flash of an optic—a sniper scope or anti-tank weapon—indicating he was about to be shot. He shot at the flash and coincidentally killed a reporter who was also in the hotel. There was controversy in the media over whether the tank commander should have used his main gun on the shooter in the hotel. Of course he should have. Shoot a bullet at me and I'll shoot artillery back at you. When your life is on the line, it's about winning. It's the same thing if someone tries to take my life outside my office. I didn't start it, so at that moment, there's no fairness or equality. I'm not trying to fight him on equal footing or fight with him; I'm trying to beat him as quickly as possible so I can walk away.

IMMINENT ATTACK: Kelly McCann (left) assumes a nonthreatening guard position when his movement is illegally arrested by a stranger (1). He visualizes striking the assailant before the man can attack him, then executes a stop-hit face mash as soon as he detects increased physical aggression (2). To create the correct hand shape, McCann orients his fingers as if he's holding a softball. The movement is executed by vaulting forward off the rear foot, thus propelling the hand into the opponent's face. McCann doesn't step forward and pull his weight, nor does he strike with his arm. Rather, he uses his whole body for power.

Photos by Thomas Sanders

BB: You must hate all the martial arts movies in which the armed hero finds himself facing an unarmed bad guy, then throws his weapon away so they can fight on equal terms.

McCann: Of course. I also hate movies in which a guy takes a slashing elbow strike across the jaw or a devastating punch to the head and keeps fighting. Movies show a lot of inaccurate things related to fighting, and they adversely affect how people shape their perception of reality on the street. There are many myths about dropping your hands, what your attacker's off hand is doing, the speed of retracting hands and one-shot stops, but in reality there are no absolutes. Any martial arts instructor who says, "If A, you do B and then C," is not being honest.

BB: That way of thinking has prompted some martial artists to adopt a philosophy that holds, "I'm going to fight fair as long as my opponent does. If he starts to fight dirty, then I'll go for his groin or eyes."

McCann: My old man used to tell me, "The only dirty fight is the one you lose." There's no such thing as dirty fighting; there's only fighting. You fight to win. And the only way you can say that is if you have a strong moral compass, if you're ethical, if you're avoidant. Anyone who naively thinks he's going to fight an enemy or criminal or anyone who truly means him harm "fairly" is going to end up an oil stain.

BB: Is there any connection between reality-based self-defense and the mixed martial arts?

McCann: Oh, yeah. I hope MMA becomes an Olympic sport. These guys are unbelievably skilled, the best in the world. MMA is out of the spectacle stage now; it's a true martial art. But not all of it applies to self-defense.

It's like in shooting. Does IPSC or IDPA shooting have anything to do with shooting a person in self-defense in Baghdad or Kabul? Functionally, yes, but there's a whole understanding of context you've got to add to it in order to benefit from training for competition. The same is true of MMA.

Technically and functionally, these guys are world-class athletes, and you should watch them and learn from them. But you need to analyze what you see: Is a technique used in the ring something you're going to pull out of your [butt] in Mauritania and use in a fight? Maybe not because the condition of the fight is going to be completely different. Under the conditions we train for, it's more about serious injury, abduction or murder—not prize money. You may be a great [grappler] until you strap on your Level-IV armor, your combat load of 180 rounds of M4 ammo, your day pack, your blow-out med kit, your drop-leg holster and so on. Are you really going to roll around on the ground with all that gear on? Will your strikes look the same? Hell, just wearing concealed armor and a concealed pistol changes everything. As an example, not only do we train students how to defeat the mount, but we also teach them how to draw and use their pistol, expandable baton and knife from the mounted position. The mind-set is completely different from normal civilian training.

If you go back to Bruce Lee and *jeet kune do*, it's all about attributes. I rely a lot on speed. I'm fast, and I can couple that with movements that generate power. I weigh only 159 pounds, but I can do things that a 250-pound guy might not be able to. Similarly, that 250-pounder is going to be more powerful than I am, so it's unlikely I can rely on strength. So I never say, "You have to do exactly what I do." That's ridiculous. Lee had it right when he threw out all the stuff that was meaningless and boiled it down to "less is more." He accepted that there are different body types and ways of thinking.

People who don't do that are part of what's wrong with combatives. There are traditionalists who learn World War II combatives verbatim, and then there are guys like me who believe in some of it but who also believe in the Philippine martial arts and jiu-jitsu—in an eclectic mix.

It's simply not about "My sensei can beat your sensei," or "Your Korean style isn't as strong as my Chinese style." None of that matters. In the end, the only thing that matters is that you believe you're training hard and the right way and that you're capable to a standard acceptable to you. It is, after all, your life. No one can say empirically that this is more devastating than that or make outrageous claims about whatever it is they teach. But if I'm going to deploy with you and your physical ability may directly affect my safety just as mine does yours, then we've got to talk. Otherwise, we don't have to agree.

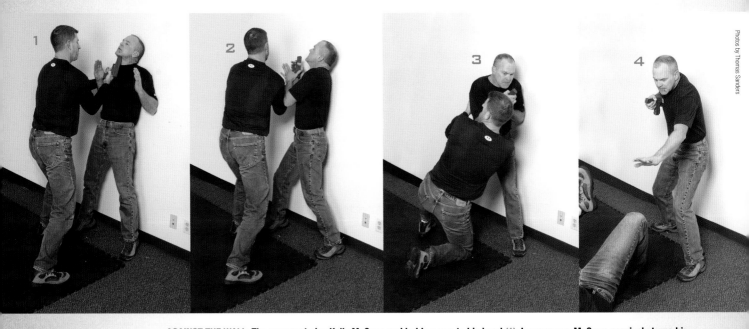

Photos by Thomas Sanders

AGAINST THE WALL: The opponent pins Kelly McCann and holds a gun to his head (1). In response, McCann passively turns his palms outward without raising his arms, which could be viewed as a sign of aggression. His action places his hands close to the pistol without telegraphing his intent. McCann explosively turns to his right and sweeps the muzzle into his outstretched right hand (2). At the same time, he moves his head away, doubling the distance between it and the muzzle. Keeping his body clear of the muzzle, he holds the attacker's wrist stationary while rotating the gun inside his hand (3). No one's grip is strong enough to prevent the technique from working. Note that McCann doesn't try to manipulate the man's wrist. Next, he rips the weapon rearward and out of the attacker's disrupted grip before executing a face smash, which knocks him backward and to the ground (4). Warning: Don't attempt a gun disarm unless you've had extensive instruction and can consistently achieve the desired result.

COMBAT IN THE REAL WORLD:
Self-Defense Secrets From Security Expert Kelly McCann
Part 2

Interview by Robert W. Young • Black Belt July 2008

BLACK BELT: DOES IT MAKE SENSE for civilians to seek out instruction in military fighting methods?

Kelly McCann: First, despite advertisements to the contrary, there are no "secret" military techniques; it's all been done before. There are different ways to put techniques together—curricula—and different training methods—regimens. What can be secret is what specific units have [with respect to] capabilities and/or equipment. A lot of the pre-emptive stuff we teach is inappropriate for civilians because they may not take the time to learn about how street violence actually occurs, what the pre-incident indicators are, and when they should and can legally use pre-emption.

BB: Is the mental side of self-defense as important as the physical side?

McCann: Fighting is 90-percent mental and 10-percent technique. It's all about having a complete, or holistic, fight mentality. This is where a dissonance starts to emerge between martial arts and combatives. Some martial arts teach you to love your enemy. I hate my enemy. When he attacks, I'm going to crush him—physically, spiritually and mentally—and I won't feel bad about it. That whole religious and philosophical side of the martial arts—I get it, but it's not for me. Combatives isn't a pretty art; it's a shovel. Its only purpose is to dig a hole. The martial arts are not shovels.

BB: Can any martial art be distilled down to its most functional techniques and then serve as that 10 percent that's physical, after which the student need only develop his mental capabilities?

McCann: That may be a bit oversimplified, but yes. The question is, Will it be distilled and by whom? If you take a guy who's studied *tai chi, tang soo do* or *taekwondo* for five or six years, he believes in his style—nobody does anything he thinks is stupid.

The bottom line is, he's completely bought into that lame "escape from the cross-wrist grab" that doesn't take into account that the attacker's off-hand is going to punch him in the head and doesn't pay attention to the way the attacker's arm will tighten and possibly prevent him from bending it into a reverse-wrist.

On the street, that guy's going to get pile-driven. I don't know what enables an instructor who's heavily invested in the totality of a particular style or system to boil it down for street use. To reduce a style to its essential, most succinct and effective methods is to admit there are techniques in it that are nonessential or ineffective. It's a *jutsu* (skill) vs. *do* (way of life) thing.

BB: Maybe a reprogramming would be required?

McCann: Maybe, except that it's the instructor who is programmed—he doesn't know what he doesn't know, and more often than not, he'll see significant change as sacrilegious. In our combatives system, it takes two years of training all the time with us to become an instructor, and then you're an employee. The combatives curriculum is composed of—if you count unarmed, stick, knife and aerosol irritant (pepper spray)—130 individual tasks, not techniques. The whole thing can be taught in five days. After that, go practice and get increasingly good and more powerful. You might come back for a refresher, but there's no advanced course.

In the martial arts business, you keep coming back for new techniques or another belt, and businesswise there's nothing wrong with that. But that's incongruent with a "less is more" practicality. Some people who gravitate toward the martial arts need that validation, and that's fine. It just shouldn't be confused with combatives.

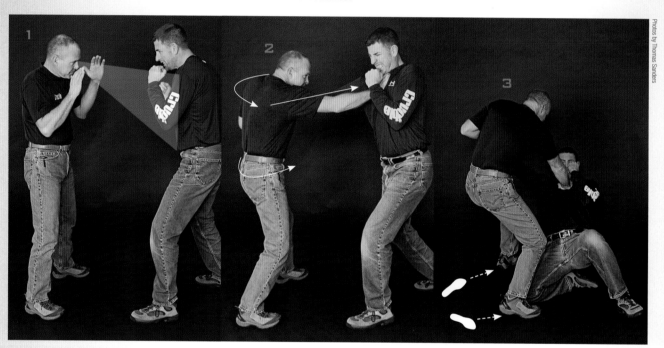

Photos by Thomas Sanders

COMBAT SCENARIO NO. 1: Kelly McCann (left) adopts a nonthreatening guard posture and focuses on his opponent's center mass so he can discern movement as early as possible (1). Despite McCann's attempts to verbally de-escalate, the opponent grabs McCann's shirt and prepares to punch him (2). McCann immediately hooks his hand, fixing it in place as he violently jerks him forward using his hips and shoulders. He simultaneously thrusts his hand forward, inserting his fingers into the opponents clavicle notch to create intense pain. McCann drives his fingers deeper, changing the angle of attack so the force is directed downward, then he hooks behind the clavicle notch—all while keeping the opponent's hand in place (3). Note how McCann shuffles forward to maintain positive pressure and maximum pain as the assailant falls backward.

BB: You said your curriculum is finite. Does that mean that once a person learns it, it's all about attributes, endurance and mind-set?

McCann: It's a matter of how smooth, how fast and how strong you can get. How quickly can you draw your folding knife and put it into action? How quickly can you deploy that collapsible baton? How far do you "vault" when you project your power during the chin jab? You have to refine the techniques so they're the best they can be.

BB: Are there any "hopeless" self-defense situations in which no technique will save you?

McCann: Absolutely. There are a lot of situations in which you don't have a chance, and it has nothing to do with what style you do or how good you are. It has to do with your situational awareness, your failure to recognize pre-incident indicators and the dynamics of the situation itself. Are you outnumbered? Are there weapons present? Are you isolated? For example, you're jumped at an ATM by two cretins with weapons. They didn't materialize out of nowhere. Where were they when you chose that particular ATM? Likely as not, you were preoccupied and didn't discern the threat. Having given up that advantage, it's nearly impossible to regain it.

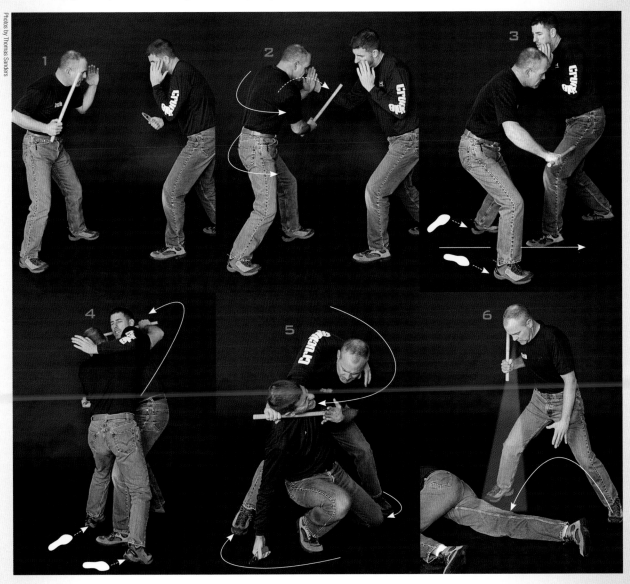

COMBAT SCENARIO NO. 2: Confronted by a man with a knife, Kelly McCann deploys his collapsible baton and assumes a rear-guard position (1). (For demonstration purposes, he's shown with a rattan stick.) As soon as the opponent slashes, McCann explosively strikes the attacking limb while he vaults slightly inside the arc of the weapon and keeps his off-hand in the guard position (2). Note how McCann rotates his hips to use his body weight to maximize the power of the strike. Next, McCann vaults in the direction of the second strike, which hits the femoral nerve (3). Moving into the opponent's space, McCann slams the stick/hand junction into the side and back of his neck—where the attacker's arm winds up is immaterial (4). As the strike lands, McCann grabs the free end of the stick and wrenches it in, putting his foe in an intensely painful neck lock. Pivoting on his left foot, McCann "opens the gate" by yanking the lock downward and to the man's rear (5). In pain and off-balance, the man falls. McCann releases the lock, chambers his weapon and focuses on the leg in case he has to follow up with a knee stomp (6).

Think of professional mixed martial artists. How hard is it for one of them, after being knocked down and put into a fugue state, to recover enough to start fighting and regain the advantage and win? Those guys train every day to do that, and even then, they can do it only about 30 percent of the time. How's the average guy going to do that after getting cold-cocked?

BB: And if you add a weapon, it's even worse.

McCann: Even without weapons, if you have five guys on one martial artist and they don't attack one at a time like they do in the movies, you're just not going to deal with that. You're probably not going to be able to deal with three on one or two on one without some help from an aerosol irritant or some other weapon. The fact is, when you fight one attacker, you can exert control. When you're faced with multiple attackers and don't have a weapon, you can't simultaneously control them.

By the way, we teach students to exploit that advantage. If you and I are deployed somewhere and you're attacked, even if you're skilled and handling it, I'm going to weigh in, too. It's all about mitigating risk, exploiting any advantage, speed and efficiency in resolving the confrontation and winning. Winning is everything when the probable consequences include injury or death.

BB: What about empty hand vs. knife or empty hand vs. gun?

McCann: You can successfully deal with those attacks, but it requires a special mentality. A guy can come at me with a knife, and given no alternative, I may disregard the knife because I know I can be inside the weapon's arc so fast and hurt him so quickly that he'll be unable to use it. He might drop it or suddenly realize he needs to get away from me—in other words, decide not to use it. Those are all forms of disarming. Disarms don't necessarily mean I have to end up with your weapon in my control.

If you could've escaped, you would've. In many of those situations, the only two choices available are to comply and hope for the best—remember that "hope" isn't a strategy—or to attack. Once you take away a person's will, the fight is over. A guy comes in and thinks he owns you, and all of a sudden he's scared stiff. If you're not willing to get to that level of commitment—turning predator into prey—you'd better not put your hand in that cage. And even then, there's no guarantee you won't end up hurt, maimed or dead.

BB: Should the law have any bearing on what a person trains to do and actually does during a self-defense encounter?

McCann: The generalized answer is, you've got to apply the "reasonable man" test. If you've lived your life lawfully and have no history of altercations, and you were avoidant on the day of the incident—if you can say, "These were the steps I took to avoid this; there was nothing else I could do"—you'll probably be OK.

But if the police find out that you had an illegal weapon in your possession prior to the assault when there was no risk, you're in trouble. In other words, if you've been carrying around an illegal weapon, stop doing that.

If you decide to use pre-emption, it must be based on pre-incident indicators you noticed and reasonably resulted in your decision to use force to protect yourself because you perceived an imminent physical threat. You've got to be able to articulate those precise pre-incident indicators and predatory behaviors to a responding police officer or in court.

If someone illegally "arrests" your movement on the street—if a guy blocks your path—he's actually assaulting you. Battery, of course, occurs once he touches you. Your rights actually start when he stops you. Now, if he's a panhandler who's just standing in your way, that's one set of thought processes. If he's a guy who comes around a corner in a back alley, that's different. But the first scenario is still dangerous. I think these statistics are still accurate: Eighty percent of all muggings

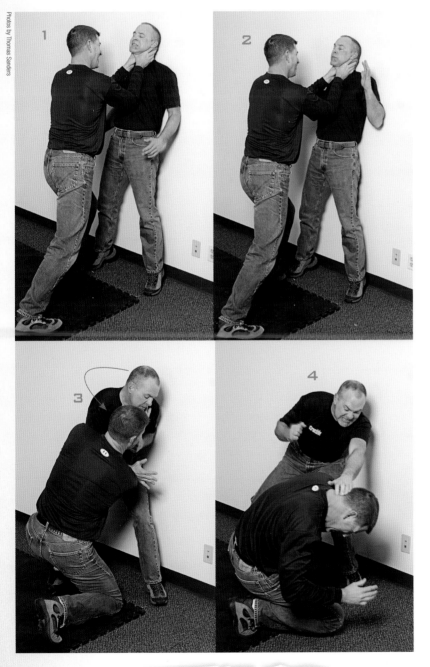

COMBAT SCENARIO NO. 3: Jack Stradley attacks Kelly McCann with a two-hand choke, pinning him against the wall (1). McCann raises his hands and formulates a plan of action before his head gets slammed into the wall or his groin gets smashed with a knee thrust (2). Using his left shoulder as a fulcrum, McCann explodes, relying on his hips and right shoulder to generate force for a forearm strike aimed at the crook of Stradley's arms (3). The blow makes contact using the outside (ulna bone) of the forearm to inflict as much pain as possible. Next, McCann re-chambers his right arm before smashing the man's head with an open-hand strike (4). Meanwhile, he prepares to stomp targets of opportunity should the need to continue his counterattack arise.

start with aggressive panhandling. It's a chance for the person to get close to you, look around and see who might be a witness, talk to you, distract you and all of a sudden he's on top of you.

BB: Do you agree that pre-emption is an important strategy for empty-hand self-defense, as well as against weapons?

McCann: Pre-emption is essential anytime someone might cold-cock you. I don't care who you are—if you turn around and take a punch to the face, you're not yourself. Your skills are diminished. Pre-emption becomes extremely important when someone menaces you. The best thing for street defense is to maintain the situational awareness to never suddenly "wake up" to find that you walked into an ambush. You have to know who's around you all the time. It's not being paranoid. It's crossing the street when you don't like what you see ahead. It's getting back into your car and finding another parking space when you don't like the look of the people who are hanging around where you wanted to park. It's being smart.

BB: Military tactics have changed so much from the 19th century to the 20th century to the 21st century. Has self-defense also changed?

McCann: Yes, and the reason is information. Information is all over the media and the Internet. You can see all the different forms of fighting now, and it wasn't always like that. For example, in the days of the Civil War, no one knew what *savate* was or thought that your feet could be used for fighting. It's possible for nonpractitioners to learn some stand-alone techniques; they can be marginally proficient with just watching television.

BB: So back then, you could take someone out with a kick to the head, and it would be totally unexpected.

McCann: I imagine so because their experience would never have indicated that people could fight like that. Nowadays, people are exposed to the mixed martial arts because it's on TV all the time and there are studios and *dojo* everywhere.

BB: Is that why Royce Gracie doesn't win the Ultimate Fighting Championship anymore?

McCann: Absolutely. People know the techniques of Brazilian *jiu-jitsu* now. The Gracie family issued a legitimate challenge to fight against their system, and they followed through. That takes big stones. They're some tough, tough guys. They're rollers, they're fit, they're mentally hard. They'll take a bunch of strikes to get you on the ground and then bend you like a pretzel. You can't take accomplishments away from anybody. You can't take them away from Dan Inosanto, from Ed Parker, from Chuck Norris. The bottom line is, the absolute statements that are made on the Internet— "So-and-so would kick so-and-so's butt!"—are ridiculous. Who are those people to say that, and how do they know it empirically? It's only their opinion.

BB: You see some UFC fighters who grew up on a farm and are naturally tough. They don't seem to care if they get punched in the face or get their arm broken in an armbar. How much of a person's fighting ability is innate, and how much can be developed?

McCann: There's a hardiness, a sturdiness that enables you to take a lot of punishment and still function. Farm life isn't easy. Excuses aren't tolerated. Stuff needs to get done—whether you're hurt or sick. There are some things you can do to develop that ethic. For example, I long-distance run. It teaches you to take a lot of pain and keep going. Pursuits that fundamentally require you to overcome mental and physical adversity are crucial.

I also believe that there's an element of meanness in being a good fighter. The martial arts try to take that out of people and instill a sense of peace, a sense that the martial arts are gentle. If it's gentle, I don't want to do it. I want to give my attacker the worst day of his life. The best fighters have that meanness, but they have it in check. It's not who they are or who they become; they unleash it when it serves their purpose. They don't wear it like a badge. It's just a necessary element to get to the most desirable outcome.

You can talk about attributes and innate qualities—agility, coordination and balance are all necessary—but the athletic side isn't as necessary as the mental side.

BB: What role does fitness play in self-defense? Is it No. 1?

McCann: You can roll hard in a grappling class for 30 minutes and think you're in shape. Then you can roll for three minutes outside a bar and feel exhausted. If you're not fit and you can't take the burst of "sprint" activity that happens in a fight, you won't fare very well. It's laughable when people who are completely out of shape think they can defend themselves.

BB: How do you develop that fighting fitness?

McCann: I think running is fabulous. When you do sprints in the middle of a long run, it really builds you up. I also think that doing some kind of fighting like judo, jiu-jitsu, grappling—anything where you hold a position for a long time and physically struggle—is essential. Sometimes you roll for five-minute intervals, and other times you go 20 minutes nonstop. You can mix it up like with the running.

BB: Anyone who's sparred nonstop for 20 or 30 minutes knows that you reach a point at which you just can't throw a roundhouse kick anymore because your legs are too tired. Are there any self-defense lessons there?

McCann: Yeah. You'll feel like you're in that situation the second minute of a fight that takes place in a supermarket parking lot. You won't have the ability to throw those techniques.

PHOTO NOTE

Without explosively jerking, applying power and torquing—and using over-the-top aggression—the techniques shown in these photos could fail. That's true for many, if not most, techniques in the martial arts. Combatives can't be broken down or segmented because each step provides a brief opportunity for an attacker to perceive and react. Although the techniques shown here were slowed down for the camera, understand that there's only one speed at which to execute them: attack speed. In each sequence, several things happen at once: movement, unloading, chambering and off-balancing, all of which work together to overwhelm the attacker. When you look at the techniques, it may not be apparent just how important aggression, commitment and determination are to success. It's essential to understand that all moves must be executed violently.

—*K.M.*

BB: Then should martial artists give up on the techniques they can't do in endurance-sparring sessions?

McCann: Less is more, man. Boil it down, then attempt it under duress.

BB: Once those techniques are decided on, what's the best way to practice them for street defense?

McCann: Change your training methodology to use startle cues. Turn your back to your partner and have him attack in a way you're not expecting when you turn around. Don't practice only in ways you feel safe. Do it between two cars. Do it on a flight of stairs. Do it with the lights on and off—and with strobe lights. Use sleep deprivation. Turn the music way up, off-the-scale loud. Bang as hard as you can stand it—the best thing about combatives is that there are no shortcuts. There's no combatives equivalent of the *"dim-mak* death touch" or other such nonsense. Prepare yourself for a snot-slinging, grueling, violent sprint to the finish, or stay at home and live your life vicariously on the Internet.

BB: If you have the fitness element, the right moves and the endurance, is strength still important?

McCann: You develop fight-applicable strength through the practice of plyometrics or explosive movements. My old man told me early on when I was a lightweight kid that I had to learn how to develop power to fight men. We're only going to be so strong depending on our physique. That's where the technique of creating a gap and rushing through it to create a collision becomes really important. You use twists, jerks, off-balances and tugs to pull the guy into your strike. It makes you exponentially more powerful.

BB: Is there a point of diminishing returns with respect to strength? If you're 125 pounds and you put on 15 pounds of muscle, you'll probably gain a lot in effectiveness. If you add another 15 pounds, will you gain as much?

McCann: Probably so, but I'm not learned enough about that to know how much increased muscle mass may restrict movement and proportionally what is optimal with respect to strength vs. flexibility vs. speed. People used to think muscleheads weren't very flexible, but now we know that's not true. One thing you can do to account for having less power is to focus on speed. If that doesn't work for you, there are alternatives. For example, I trained a guy for a year, and he was technically perfect but slow. He just wasn't effective on his feet. His way around that limitation was to get his opponent on the ground. He became really proficient by focusing on his attributes—a great "ground sense" and the ability to apply leverage—rather than trying to rely on techniques that require hand speed.

BB: For civilians, how important is verbal de-escalation?

McCann: It's great for a certain kind of fight. The easiest way to respond to a potential threat is to walk away. But those fights, although they happen frequently, aren't nearly as injurious as when a person comes over to talk and then tries to take your head off. There's no de-escalation option. He's already made the decision to fight before he presented himself to you.

BB: Does that mean that even if you're going to try to talk your way out of a fight, you should plan your response?

McCann: Mentally, when you're negotiating, you should have already "hit" the other person. You need to cross that threshold of commitment before he does. He hasn't hit you because he's still talking. He's still trying to work himself up to the point where he can hit you. Outwardly, you're trying to de-escalate, giving him what he wants, giving him a sense of control. But you're ready. Defending, by its very nature, is losing. You can't win through defense. Attack, attack, attack.

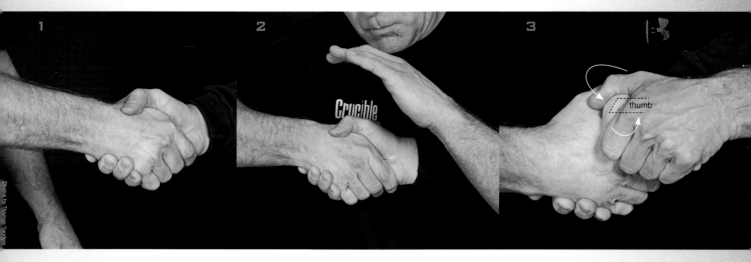

COMBAT SCENARIO NO. 4: Some altercations start when a passive aggressor disguises his intent by reaching out to shake the hand of his victim. The victim attempts to free his hand, but the man tightens his grip. One method of escape relies on thumb manipulation. Kelly McCann jerks his opponent forward by pulling his arm and simultaneously stepping out with his left foot to position his hips perpendicular to the other man's hips (1-2). At the same time, McCann whips his left arm over the opponent's arm, which hyperextends the limb and places him out of reach of a punch. Meanwhile, McCann prepares to "wipe" the man's thumb. The action entails grabbing the digit to isolate it, then bending and compressing it (3). The assailant will react by rising to his toes, which enables McCann to control him with pain compliance or throw him to the ground by leveraging the trapped arm while jerking his left shoulder down and to the rear.

BB: Earlier, you said there are no secrets in self-defense.

McCann: That's right—maybe "proprietary" is a reasonable word to use but not "secret." It's all in the training methods and how you put your skills together. Also, it's how you use the "equipment" you have. The notion that there are literally "classified techniques of self-defense" is ridiculous— and that's coming from someone who's lived and worked in the "classified" world all my adult professional life.

BB: How should people develop the ability to use their equipment, their attributes? Should they form a group of like-minded individuals and go all-out? Should they create realistic scenarios? Should they attend courses taught by ex-military instructors who have lots of real-world experience?

McCann: Not necessarily. Those options could be a turnoff to people who are ... mild mannered or meek. Nonassertive or passive people need to know how to fight, too—perhaps more so because they have a higher likelihood of being victimized—but you can't bully or beat them into learning it. You have to find their motivational button. How you develop a timid person mentally into ac- cepting—better still, desiring—hard, realistic training is difficult. A significant percentage of the time, it's impossible. Our student group comes with an inclination toward violence, so we deal with that situation less often than martial arts instructors, but we have been confronted with it.

Primarily, we've learned that it's about empowerment. If you can get the student to honestly achieve proficiency in one or two tasks—not the perception of proficiency but real proficiency—you can use that realization as an enabler. Success begets success. You have to really work to get their commitment to sacrifice for tangible gains, assuring them that ultimately they'll be able to exert more control over their safety than they ever thought possible.

Trying to instill the resolute will to survive, to risk being hurt in order to hurt—or even the ability to hurt at all—isn't easy. You have to make a conscious decision to fight. You're going to be alone when that decision must be made. You'll be without peer support or encouragement. It's a very personal, tough thing that some find easy and some find abhorrent.

When you're a kid, you're happy-go-lucky. In adolescence, you start noticing that some kids turn mean and are capable of cruelty. By that point in your life, you need to have made personal decisions that enable you to cultivate the capacity to deal with physical manifestations of meanness and cruelty. In my opinion, everyone should get to that point in order to feel secure. Some people, though, have the attitude that if something happens, it was just meant to be. They refuse to acknowledge that they had any responsibility to influence or control the situation. You might as well paint "victim" on their forehead.

Others think, I'm going to take care of me and mine!

THE CRIMINAL MIND:
Know Your Enemy!

by Ernest Emerson • Black Belt December 2006

LET'S TAKE A LOOK AT TWO FIGHTS:

1. The lights are bright, and the cheers and whistles of the crowd sound as if you're hearing them through a long cardboard tube. You're sweating. The gate behind you swings shut, and you look toward the crowd but see only spotlights. Your mind races, but you stay focused. Your hands tremble, and you begin breathing deep to get more oxygen into your blood. Looking across the ring, you see him. He looks mad, focused and intense, hopping from one foot to the other with a fighter's rhythm. You think, I'm ready. Then you hear the ref shout, "Touch gloves!" You step to the center of the ring.

2. It's 10:30 p.m., and you just turned onto the street that leads to your apartment. You locate an empty parking spot, but it looks like a tight fit. As you jockey your car into position, your thoughts drift to the argument you just had with your boss. Grabbing your briefcase, you open the door to step out and—wham! It's not a noise; it's more like a flash of white light that drops you to your knees. Your right hand shoots reflexively to the back of your head. Then something hits the middle of your back and drives your face into the pavement. You hear a sound, a snarl crossed with a grunt, barely human. It gets louder each time you're hit. Again and again something explodes into your face and ribs. Finally, you're shoved against the cold blacktop. The blows stop, and you hear running footsteps. Then the world fades to black.

Photo courtesy of Ernest Emerson

Most street fighters will try to ambush their victims—whether it's with a punch, a tackle or a knife thrust. That makes it difficult for a martial artist to practice fending off an assailant in a realistic scenario.

WELCOME TO THE STREET

Most martial artists think they're training to defend against that kind of street attack, but they're not. Although arguments over how the average martial artist could beat the average person are common, a street fighter isn't an average person. He's a ruthless thug who's probably done prison time, might have killed someone and won't hesitate to stomp your face into hamburger after he knocks you out. He's by no means a guy most martial artists would want to meet in a parking lot.

I've run across several such guys in my career; fortunately, I didn't have to deal with them physically. I have, however, witnessed the brutal and shocking results of their actions. They won't just beat you; they'll kill you if they have the chance. Are you prepared?

Because it's hard to know what a street fighter will do, it's difficult to prepare. There is, however, a lot you can do, and it starts with the old military axiom: Proper planning leads to perfect performance.

Another military saying also applies: If you prepare for the worst, you can handle most other situations. To be able to fend off a deadly attack, you need to practice all the basics—conditioning, drills, sparring and so on—but you also need to know what you're up against so you can be ready physically and mentally.

That brings up a crucial question: What makes a street fighter so effective? While searching for an answer, I devised the following list of eight attributes, attitudes and actions. It'll help you know what to expect and what to incorporate into your training.

HE AIMS TO AMBUSH YOU

Chances are, your assailant will surprise you—whether it's with an unprovoked punch, an unseen tackle or an out-of-the-blue ambush. In any street fight, the odds are stacked against you, and this is where it starts. It won't be a you-want-to-step-outside bar fight because he has no sense of fair play. He'll hit you when you're distracted or jump you in a restroom. If you're not "switched on," as the Brits say, you'll never see it coming.

This is the first big advantage the street fighter has: He knows he's going to attack, but you don't.

HE'S WILLING TO DO ANYTHING

Martial artists love to hypothesize about what they'd do to stop a bad guy—how they'd tear open an attacker's cheek, bite off his nose or crush his throat. Would you be able to do it? Could you do it without hesitating even for an instant? You have to because your opponent sure won't hesitate.

Because we're the good guys, we're at a disadvantage in this respect. We're unwilling to fight dirty, to cheat to win. They don't have rules, but we do. It doesn't matter whether they come from religion, family, society or sports; we've been imbued with morality, fair play, honor and respect for other human beings. Bad guys don't have a moral braking system like we do.

HE'S DONE THIS BEFORE

He's done this before, or he's had it done to him. Experience is a great teacher; unfortunately, it doesn't differentiate between good and bad behavior. When a street fighter stomps someone's head into the ground, he's playing his game and he's used to it.

HE'LL USE EXTREME VIOLENCE

If we're lucky, most of us will never encounter extreme physical violence. For those who experience it, especially the first time, it can have extreme effects.

The average criminal is well-acquainted with fighting. He's probably used hundreds of attacks and had them used against him.

Reactions can range from a deer-in-the-headlights freeze-up to on-the-spot nausea. The freeze-up, coupled with a gut-wrenching feeling that mixed fear and dread, was exploited by the September 11 hijackers when they killed flight attendants in full view of the passengers.

Bad guys are usually the result of a violent past. Not only have they experienced violence before, but some of them actually enjoy it. They know they're different from us, and they know that works to their advantage.

In training, it's important to use scenarios that elicit surprise and fear so you know what it feels like—before you experience it for the first time in a fight. The more realistic you make your combat training, the higher the probability that you'll survive actual combat.

Extreme violence is the trademark of the street thug, Ernest Emerson says, and martial artists must be ready to reply in kind.

HE HAS ATTITUDE AND INTENT

When an enraged biker decides to attack you, he does it with an attitude (anger, ferociousness, vengeance) and intent (your complete and utter destruction). On the other hand, you'll be fighting defensively with no intent—with just your survival instinct. Until you reverse this reactionary mode, you'll be doing just that: reacting. You must start acting—fighting back—as quickly as possible. Being in the reactive mode for even a few seconds gives him enough time to inflict grave bodily harm.

Unfortunately, most martial arts are taught using a reactive premise: If he strikes, I'll block and counter. They're more defensive than offensive. Consequently, you must focus on enhancing your offensive and pre-emptive abilities. Once again, scenario training is the ticket. It'll teach you how to turn the tables on a street fighter. Key point: If you practice only defensive counters, you're giving him the first shot.

HE'LL BE ARMED

A veteran street fighter will use anything and everything to gain the advantage. That means he probably won't engage you unless he has a weapon. Whether it's a gun, knife, pool cue, beer bottle, pipe or rock, he'll have something in his hand or readily available. Lesson to be learned: Start practicing your weapon defense.

HE WON'T BE ALONE

Rest assured that your attacker probably won't operate solo. He'll have an accomplice to set you up, distract

Street fighters are usually armed. Even if you don't see a weapon, you should assume one is present and be ready to deal with it.

AVOID RATHER THAN FIGHT

Most street attacks will involve odds stacked against you—from the number of assailants to the distribution of weapons. You'll need every ounce of resolve and willpower you possess, on top of all your physical capabilities, to survive.

That's exactly why most martial arts instructors wisely advise students to avoid trouble whenever possible. Three of the best ways to do that are to stay alert, use common sense and listen to your gut feeling.

If you ever find yourself thinking, I shouldn't go into that bar with all those Harleys out front, listen to that voice. You're using all three aforementioned tools.

—E.E.

you or help him beat you down. Contrary to what many people say, it's not because thugs are cowards. In fact, many of them are brave when their actions are viewed objectively. I've seen some bad guys face five or six formidable opponents and not back up one inch. They travel in packs because experience tells them that the odds are better when it's two, three or 10 against one.

HE WON'T BE IN SHAPE

He doesn't have to be, but it doesn't matter. After all, this is a fight, not a match. Fights don't last long—seconds, maybe. They're nowhere near the duration of a kickboxing round.

How many punches can you throw in 10 seconds? How many stomp kicks can you deliver in five seconds? That's usually all it takes. Rage, fury, adrenaline and illegal drugs can carry the most out-of-shape, overweight thug long enough to maim or kill another human being.

These eight characteristics are some, but not all, of the traits that give the street fighter his edge. Knowing them should convince you that you must be able to fight until you can prevail or escape. The next time you work out, review your routine with these points in mind. If you see any gaps in your arsenal, fill them before it's too late.

Photo courtesy of Ernest Emerson

The best way to steel yourself against the adrenaline rush that accompanies a real attack is to engage in scenario training designed to surprise the participants, says Ernest Emerson (right).

WILL YOUR WEAPONS DEFENSE GET YOU KILLED?
Reality-Based Fighter Shows You the
Right Way to Neutralize a Knife or Gun Attack

by E. Lawrence • Black Belt June 2009

DEFENSE AGAINST WEAPONS has always been a heated topic among martial artists and self-defense practitioners. Opinions vary based on style, background and experience, but the seriousness of the subject requires that everyone think about it because trying an ineffective technique can get you killed.

One critic of commonly taught weapons defenses is Montreal-based Richard Dimitri, founder of *senshido*. He notes that many instructors would rather modify reality to fit their system than adapt their system to fit real life. Example: the partner who attacks in a manner that makes the defense work or who holds his weapon in a position that makes it easy to execute the prescribed disarm.

In contrast, real attacks involve chaotic, ballistic motions, and real attackers move rapidly before, during and after the assault. They retract their knives after thrusting and slashing and follow up with more thrusts and slashes. When they hold their blades stationary to rob or threaten you, they rarely do so in a manner that lends itself to picture-perfect disarming.

The first step toward overcoming that deficiency, Dimitri says, is to restructure your training so your partner really tries to "stab" or "shoot" you. It's also crucial to create the emotional conditions that exist in a real assault. To do that, you need a partner who issues verbal threats and who behaves and reacts the way real criminals do.

The first component of an effective defense is awareness—not just awareness of your general environment but also awareness of pre-assault indicators and the rituals of violence, Dimitri says. You must be able to recognize the situational and behavioral elements that precede an armed attack, along with the body language and movements.

Before attempting to disarm a thug, it helps to distract him. To do that successfully, you must first figure out what he wants because that will determine what you need to say or do. Dimitri recommends asking the assailant a question that forces him to think, thus creating a momentary hesitation. It will permit you to use your hands in a manner that's consistent with the behavior he expects from someone who's terrified. What appears to be a pleading gesture on your part can be an excellent way to maneuver your hands closer to his weapon.

When it comes to physical responses, Dimitri advocates learning principles rather than specific defenses. Planning to use specific defenses is problematic, he says, for two reasons: You need to learn a technique for every possible situation, and remembering and effectively executing the right technique in a split second is nearly impossible.

The shortcoming is exacerbated by instructors who create unnatural situations in the *dojo* to make their techniques work. For example, if your partner attacks you in a realistic manner, with his knife moving quickly and changing from a slash to a thrust or from one angle to another, it's unrealistic to expect that you can discern the angle of attack and apply the appropriate response. That's why you need to have general principles that work against a variety of offenses.

Some of Dimitri's knife-defense strategies depend on whether the weapon is stationary or moving, while others apply to all situations. Common to both is the need to avoid getting cut in a vital area (neck, heart, inner thigh, etc.), even if it means placing a less-critical body part in the path of the blade.

Next, he says, you must clear your body. That means ascertaining how the knife has to move to hurt you and then shifting in the opposite direction to get out of harm's way. You should also attempt to seize the attacker's arm and pin it against something to stabilize the weapon and prevent it from damaging you. Securing the knife need not occupy both your hands for the rest of the fight; once you have control of it, you can briefly let go with one hand and strike a vital area. As soon as you do that, however, you should go back to securing the weapon.

Finally, you need to neutralize him using the most effective means available. Aim to inflict maximum injury so he concentrates on the pain rather than on attacking you.

Martial artists love to argue over whether you should expect to get cut during a knife attack. Although some claim it's defeatist to tell yourself you'll be injured, Dimitri says you should anticipate getting sliced so you don't freeze or panic if it happens. He relates a story about getting slashed across the chest with a knife back when he was new to the martial arts. He stopped to look at the gash before re-engaging. Afterward, he realized that if the knifer had been more competent, he'd have taken

Photos by Anthony Luktan

DEFENSE AGAINST A KNIFE:
Richard Dimitri is pinned against a wall at knifepoint (1). Feigning fear, he distracts the attacker with dialogue, then momentarily secures the knife while kneeing him in the groin (2). Maintaining control of the weapon, Dimitri maneuvers behind the attacker and elbows him in the back of the head (3). Without letting go of the knife hand, the martial artist digs his fingers into his eyes.

advantage of Dimitri's momentary distraction and finished him.

Don't buy into claims that you'll pass out or die if you get stabbed in a specific spot, Dimitri says. If it happens, it happens, but you can often keep on fighting. How does that translate to training? Never quit. Even if you sustain a "fatal" stab with a rubber knife, continue to fight back. On the street, people survive knife attacks, some of which involve multiple stabs and slashes, all the time.

Many of the principles Dimitri teaches for nullifying a static attack hold true for knives and firearms. Whether you're held at knifepoint or gunpoint, it's essential to employ a passive stance that has your hands moving slowly in a manner that's congruous with someone who's scared. During this time, your adversary will be extremely aware and tense while he measures your ability to resist. If you make any sudden moves, you could be stabbed or shot.

One of the most important parts of weapons defense against a static attack is playing along with the attacker to cultivate a false sense of security and distract him. Efforts to verbally de-escalate the tension will likely lower his guard and bolster his ego. Then, if you need to get physical, he'll be less prepared to react.

This concept forms the foundation of Dimitri's behavioral approach to self-defense, and it's emphasized throughout senshido.

If you find yourself facing a static knife attack at a distance, running away is usually the best option. Grabbing an improvised weapon is also good, as long as doing so doesn't leave you open to your opponent's rush.

KNIFE DEFENSE: When he and a companion are accosted by a man with a knife, Richard Dimitri (center) engages the aggressor with dialogue (1). While he's momentarily distracted, Dimitri seizes his knife arm (2). He redirects the weapon to stab the attacker (3), then gouges his eyes (4). Next, Dimitri executes an elbow smash to the face (5). Still controlling the knife, the defender pulls the attacker down into his rising knee thrust (6).

Because you can't realistically expect to discern the nature of a moving knife attack and then select and execute the proper defense, it's even more important to follow Dimitri's belief that principles trump techniques. On the subject of trying to control the weapon versus attacking the attacker, he leans toward controlling the weapon. However, if that's not immediately doable, you should switch to a plan that takes advantage of whatever your opponent makes available—attacking his weapon hand, overwhelming him with strikes or decimating him with the senshido "shredder" technique.

When facing a dynamic knife attack, assume a posture that makes it hard for the blade to reach your vital areas, Dimitri says. Your chin should be tucked and your shoulders raised to protect your neck and throat. Your arms should be up in a boxing-style stance with the backs of your arms toward the knife and your hands closed.

Your ability to block his offensive moves is but a minor obstacle for the assailant, Dimitri says. After his strikes are stopped a few times—at most—he'll start stabbing from another angle. That's why Dimitri advocates jamming his arm against his body or otherwise grabbing it and anchoring it to arrest the knife's movement. A firm anchor involves wrapping the limb and cupping the elbow while pinning it to your body. As soon as the knife is stabilized, pummel the attacker to put him on the defensive. Then he'll be more concerned with avoiding what you're doing to him than with attacking you.

Jamming shouldn't be confused with blocking, parrying or passing. Jamming entails slamming your forearms or hands into the attacker's knife arm with the goal of immobilizing it. Jams are preferred because they're gross-motor movements and can be used on a variety of attacks.

Ideally, one of your hands should jam the biceps of his thrusting arm and the other his wrist. Make sure you drive forward with your whole body. Using only your arms is weak and leaves you overextended and vulnerable.

Moving in to jam the knife might get you cut, but it offers the best chance of controlling the weapon, thus minimizing the overall damage while getting you into position for the shredder. The shredder is a spontaneous fusillade of gross-motor attacks such as eye gouges, face rakes, ear and nose rips, bites, hair pulls, neck wrenches and throat crushes. The onslaught can also include elbows, head butts and other close-range assaults.

As soon as you pin the knife arm against his body, use one hand to keep it there. With the other one, attack his eyes or throat.

If the knife isn't within jamming range, Dimitri says, you must attack him as viciously as possible. Your aim is to make him more concerned with defending himself than with stabbing you, thus reversing the predator/prey mentality.

If he's outside "traffic range"—the distance at which both parties are close enough to hit each other—remain far enough back to force him to telegraph his intentions before he can get to you.

If he's close but not lunging toward you, Dimitri favors throwing quick, low-line kicks to get him to back off or to distract him before you drive forward with a jamming technique. Kick with the leg that's closest to him.

Against a firearm, remember that you're facing a weapon that has an extended range, which makes it more dangerous in some respects. However, because the bullet can come out of the barrel only one way, the muzzle must be pointed at you to inflict damage. And because a gun is held steady when it's used—the attacker doesn't wave it around like a knife—it's easier to grab or divert at close range.

Photos by E. Lawrence

DEFENSE AGAINST A GUN: An assailant grabs Richard Dimitri and threatens him with a gun (1). Dimitri feigns compliance and starts to hand over his car keys (2) before dropping them (3). With his hands strategically placed near the weapon, he grabs it and points the muzzle in a safe direction (4). Maintaining control of the gun, Dimitri slams his forehead into the attacker's face (5), then strips it from his hand (6). Dimitri immediately follows up with a debilitating face smash (7).

You must be close to the gunman before you can disarm him. If the firearm isn't within reach, you'll need to bridge the gap using dialogue. Say something that will elicit his interest, then distract him and get him to lower his guard. Remain passive; don't challenge or threaten him.

For example, you might point to your pocket and say, "My spare cash is here; I'll give it all to you if you want." Meanwhile, you edge closer to the gunman, making sure to move your hands in a manner that's consistent with being scared while you offer him the money.

Then grab the gun and direct the muzzle away from you. If you're near other people, try not to point it in their direction, either. That consideration is often overlooked in the dojo, where disarms may be effected without concern for bystanders.

Although a knife defense that involves grabbing the attacker's wrist is permissible because it's tough for the opponent to stab, such a strategy won't work for gun defense. The reason: Even if you control the wrist, he can probably bend it enough to shoot you. You must seize the hand or the weapon. Once that's done, explode with counterattacks.

Dimitri knows that when it comes to weapons defense, there are no guarantees. However, if you concentrate on the facets of fighting described earlier, you'll be better able to turn the tables on an attacker when you otherwise wouldn't have stood a chance.

GUN GRABBING:
The Israeli System of Haganah
Teaches State-of-the-Art Handgun Disarms!

by Randy S. Proto • Black Belt April 2006

JUST AS EVERY ORGANISM ON EARTH evolves, so too does self-defense. Back when our cavemen ancestors wielded crude clubs and stone axes, there was surely a set of defensive maneuvers that served to counter the overhead swing and whatever other attacks Cro-Magnon man used. In the Iron Age when mankind started using swords and knives to wage war, people were forced to design a different set of defenses to nullify the fighting methods associated with those more advanced weapons.

Now, in many countries around the world, the weapon of choice for criminals is the gun—specifically, the handgun. Because close-range handgun combat is a fairly recent development for society, not every martial art has kept its curriculum up to date with respect to gun defense. There is, however, a reality-based self-defense system that focuses a substantial part of its curriculum on disarms and continually fine-tunes its strategies and techniques with the latest research from the field. Its name is *haganah,* and its founder is Mike Lee Kanarek.

Kanarek, a former Israeli commando, knows that being threatened by a gunman is among the most stressful encounters you'll ever experience. Desensitizing your body to handle an unarmed attack via rigorous *dojo* training is one thing, but preparing for the possibility of an armed assault requires a methodology that's not found in most martial arts schools.

The requisite level of physical and mental preparation can be obtained only from an art devised by someone who's experienced such conflicts. That brings us back to haganah, an integrated and balanced system of defensive tactics for all settings, the evolutionary end product of Israeli self-defense and close-quarters combat. It blends *hisardut* and other arts with tactics and strategies from the nation's special-operations units. The result is an eclectic system that takes defense against armed and unarmed attackers to a new level of effectiveness.

KEEPING IT REAL

Kanarek believes that learning gun defense without first having knowledge of firearms—how they work, what they sound like and how they're used in the commission of crimes—is like learning to box without sparring. You might be able to perform drills, but in the ring when you get hit, everything changes. Your ability to implement what you've learned plunges the moment you get hit—unless you've been conditioned through contact fighting.

The same is true for gun defense: You won't be able to use what you know if you go into shock the moment you hear a bang.

Consistent with its origin and philosophy, haganah requires students to learn how to shoot. And it's not target shooting they engage in; it's combat shooting. They drill under stress with different types of guns to desensitize their nervous systems to the presence of firearms—their actions, their sounds and their smells.

GUN BASICS

Haganah gun defense is predicated on five key points that are true of virtually all firearms:

1. A gun discharges when its trigger is pulled—provided the safety is off and a round is in the chamber.
2. It takes very little pressure to pull the trigger.
3. A gun fires the bullet in essentially a straight line toward whatever object it's pointing at when the trigger is pulled (line of fire).
4. A gun is extremely loud. If one discharges nearby, you'll be startled and your ears will ring—even if you expect it.
5. If you interfere with the normal operation of certain parts of a gun during the firing process, it'll

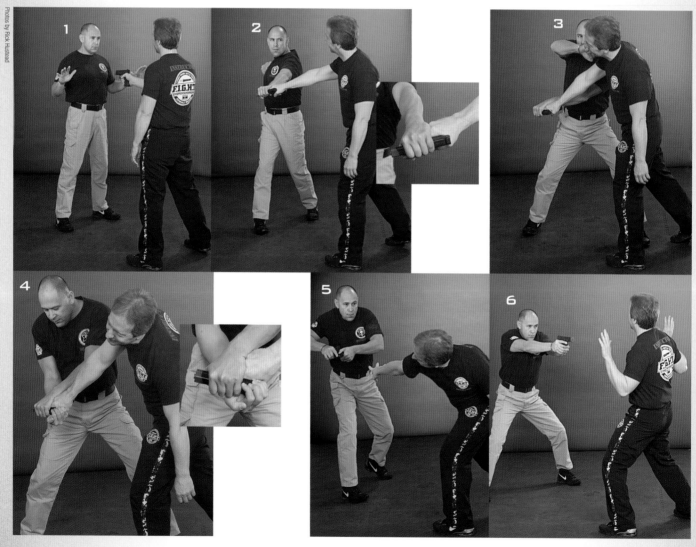

Photos by Rick Hustead

BASIC DISARM: When Mike Lee Kanarek is threatened by a gunman, he raises his hands to the height of the weapon and feigns compliance (1). He then twists his torso to move off the line of fire and simultaneously grabs the gun near the trigger guard (2). At this point, the gun will probably fire. Next, Kanarek steps in, pulls the gun down and away, and strikes (3). He then uses his free hand to grab the rear of the slide (4). To take away the weapon, he steps back and rotates it out of the attacker's grasp (5), after which he opens the distance, racks the gun to clear it and controls the scene (6).

probably jam, rendering it incapable of firing again until the problem is fixed. On a semiautomatic weapon, that involves stopping the slide from slamming backward upon discharge and then being propelled forward to chamber another round. The result is an empty chamber, which means no follow-up shot can be made without recocking the weapon.

A basic assumption taught in haganah is that if a person threatens you with a gun, it's better to take away the weapon than to leave your life in his hands. If that's not possible or you don't feel confident, you'll have to comply until another opportunity presents itself.

Haganah's definition of a gun threat is a situation in which a person points a firearm at you and makes a demand in exchange for not shooting you. To successfully execute a disarm, the gun must be within reach or you must be able to cause it to be so. If your attacker maintains his distance, the best technique in the world won't help you.

SIX PRINCIPLES

Haganah gun disarms are based on six primary principles:

1. **Mind-set:** The assailant has a demand, which is why he's threatening you instead of shooting you. Because he's heavily armed, he probably won't expect you to act against him. Feign compliance if you can. Raise your hands to the level of the gun or lower to indicate that you'll do what he wants. This action will reduce his stress level and bolster his perception that he'll get his way. It'll also cause his brain to process what you say. All that will give you a momentary advantage because while he thinks, you can act.

IN A VEHICLE: The assailant positions his weapon to the side of Mike Lee Kanarek's head (1). Kanarek feigns compliance until he's ready to act: He uses his left arm to direct the gun away from his head and toward the attacker (2). He then uses his right hand to grab his own left hand or the attacker's hand (3). Rotating the weapon up and away strips it from the man's grasp (4). Kanarek completes the technique by racking the gun while keeping it out of the attacker's reach (5) and using it to fend him off until he can exit the vehicle (6).

2. **Primary Danger:** In a gun attack, the primary danger is being in the line of fire. Your preferred course of action during the execution of a disarm is to get off the line, but it's acceptable to redirect it. Obviously, you can do both if the situation permits. Just don't ever move in such a way that you put your body back in the line of fire. Disarms are categorized by the initial angle and height of the line of fire—whether it's from the front, side or back, and whether it's to the head, body or some other target. Because the line of fire will likely change as you execute any disarm, you must move in a way that minimizes collateral damage should the gun go off. Line of fire is a simple principle, but as you become more skilled, you'll see that it's often affected by the environment (obstacles, bystanders and so on).

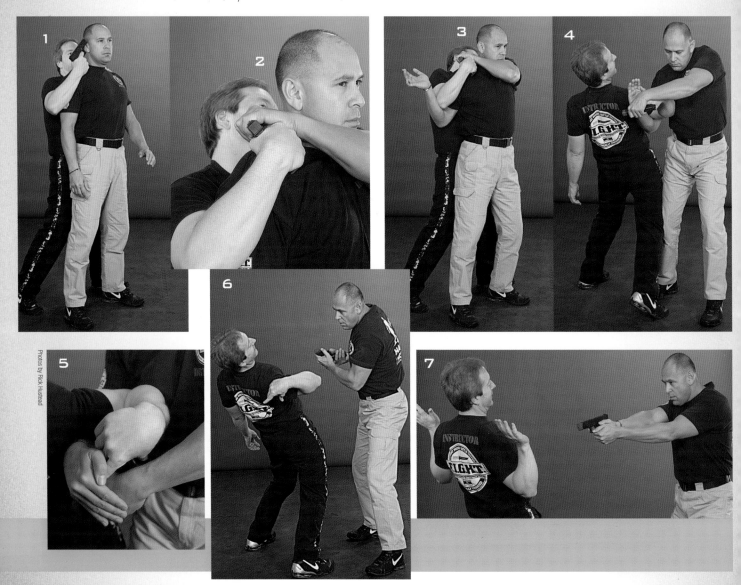

Photo by Rick Hustead

REAR ATTACK: The gunman approaches from behind and places his weapon against the side of Mike Lee Kanarek's head (1). With his right arm pinned, Kanarek is forced to use his left, so he sneaks it up and across his chest until he can grab the gun and redirect the line of fire away from his head (2). Then, if it discharges, the attacker will likely be neutralized. Next, Kanarek wraps his right arm under the attacker's elbow (3) and turns to his right (4) so he can grab his own right hand with his left (5). To effect the disarm, he steps past the attacker while "pumping" the gun down and away (6). With the man off-balance and unarmed, Kanarek is in control (7).

3. **Weapon Control:** You must quickly gain and maintain control of the gun. Assume the assailant will struggle to regain control of it, usually by pulling away. Controlling the gun typically means holding it around the barrel near the trigger guard. Grasping it closer to the end of the barrel is tactically weak for several reasons: Overlapping the muzzle becomes more likely, compensated barrels can burn you, and the rotation of the cylinder of a revolver won't be interfered with and therefore won't prevent it from firing again.

4. **Short-Circuiting:** If possible, interrupt or short-circuit the gunman's physical and mental flow by striking him without disconnecting from him and possibly losing control of the weapon. In haganah, that's called "short-circuiting," and it's necessary if you wish to effect a disarm once you've seized the gun. While he may be mentally short-circuited merely by your grabbing his weapon or by its unexpected discharge, it's important to keep him off-balance by striking him. Your purpose isn't to inflict serious damage; it's to keep him stunned while you initiate the disarm.

5. **Firearms Operation:** During a disarm, assume that the gun is operable and prepare yourself for the effects of a discharge. Upon gaining possession of the weapon, assume that it's jammed and has to be cleared (the unfired round is extracted) for it to be operable again. As mentioned earlier, without a working knowledge of how the most common firearms operate, you probably won't be able to use the assailant's gun against him if need be—or even know if you *can* use it. Further, a lack of knowledge could lead you to inadvertently discharge it, thus putting bystanders at risk.

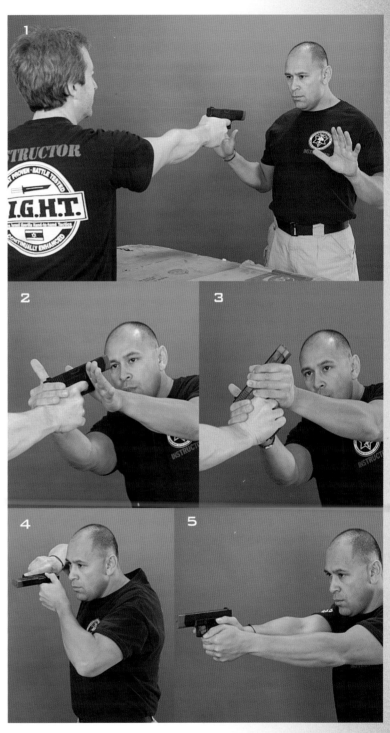

CLUTTERED ENVIRONMENT: With an obstacle in between, Mike Lee Kanarek faces the assailant (1). He immediately reaches out and grabs the gun with both hands (2) so he can twist it to the side and tilt it upward (3). The disarm occurs when Kanarek's left hand pushes and his right pulls, leveraging the firearm from the man's grip. After clearing and cocking the weapon (4), the *haganah* practitioner uses it to keep the assailant at bay (5).

6. **Exit Strategy:** After gaining possession of the gun, think of an exit strategy. Open up the distance and control the scene, or escape. If that's not possible, such as when you're in a car, you'll need to employ tactics that account for the close quarters. No matter which option you select, do so with a detailed knowledge of your state's laws pertaining to the use of firearms in a self-defense situation.

Conclusion

In any combat situation involving guns, the environment and the actions of you, your assailant and even innocent bystanders can affect the outcome of the encounter by presenting you with a unique set of challenges. The haganah tactics and principles described in this article will bolster your ability to master a defensive strategy that could save your life.

In any armed threat, particularly one involving a firearm, only you can decide the appropriate course of action. Having tactically sound training and tactics will shore up your self-confidence, which is exactly what you need to act forcefully and prevail.

THE ULTIMATE THREAT:
Krav Maga's State-of-the-Art Methods for Neutralizing Gun Attacks

by John Whitman • Black Belt November 2003

CONSIDER THESE TWO SCENARIOS:

Scenario No. 1

It's late at night. You're walking to your car in a parking structure lit by a few dim bulbs spaced too far apart. Your mind is occupied, and you're obviously not as aware of your surroundings as you ought to be. Without warning, a man steps out of the shadows. You can't see his face, but you can see the semi-automatic pistol in his hand. It hovers a few feet away, pointing at your chest.

"Give me your car keys now!" he orders.

Startled out of your thoughts and frightened by the gun, you dig into your pocket for your keys.

"Give them to me!" he commands, and you obey.

"Back up. Get back!" Again, you do as you're told.

The gunman snatches the keys, gets in your car and drives away.

Scenario No. 2

It's late at night. You're walking to your car in a parking structure lit by a few dim bulbs spaced too far apart. Your mind is occupied, and you're obviously not as aware of your surroundings as you ought to be. Without warning, a man steps out of the shadows. You can't see his face, but you can see the semi-automatic pistol in his hand. It hovers a few feet away, pointing at your chest.

"Give me your car keys now!" he orders.

Startled out of your thoughts and frightened by the gun, you dig into your pocket for your keys.

"Give them to me!" he commands, and you obey.

"Back up. Get back!" Again, you do as you're told.

The gunman snatches the keys, then backs away and shouts, "Now get in the trunk!"

The first scenario is a clear argument for complying with a gunman's demands. A handgun represents a significant threat to your life. If you can maintain your safety by giving him what he wants, do it. Your car, your wallet and your jewelry are meaningless. Going home to your family is everything.

The actions described in scenario No. 1 are replayed on the streets of America every day. Unfortunately, so are those described in scenario No. 2. You can cooperate with an armed assailant and give him everything he asks for—and still end up in mortal danger.

The worst part is that you may never know which scenario you're facing until it is too late. This simple, unnerving fact is the clearest reason for including realistic gun defenses in your defensive-tactics system.

Krav maga, the official hand-to-hand combat system of the Israeli Defense Forces, includes some of the most practical and effective techniques in existence—techniques that are relied on by soldiers and police officers who face armed threats day in and day out.

The methods krav maga teaches for gun defense allow you to create responses that work in a wide variety of circumstances. That reduces the number of techniques you must learn and remember, which results in a shorter training time and faster application under stress. For instance, krav maga uses the same technique when a gun is placed anywhere in front of you, whether it is touching you or not. The same technique, with very minor adjustments in body defense, works when the gun is pointed at your forehead, under your chin or at the side of your head.

All krav maga gun techniques employ four basic principles: Redirect the line of fire, control the weapon, counterattack and disarm. Often these four principles will overlap. For instance, controlling the weapon and counterattacking frequently take place at the same time. For you to successfully use a gun defense in the gravest extreme, you must understand and be able to implement all four principles.

GUN-ATTACK DEFENSE: The defender (left) faces a gun threat from the front (1). He leads with his left hand, redirecting the weapon with minimal movement (2). Note how that action also creates a body defense and how the defender's weight begins to shift forward only after the hand movement. The defender then bursts forward, putting his weight in and down on the gun while he punches the assailant's face (3). After taking the weapon out of the assailant's hand (4), he retreats to safety (5). (The distance was shortened for photographic reasons.)

REDIRECT THE LINE OF FIRE

A good defense against any threat must first address the primary danger, and clearly the most immediate danger from a gun is getting shot. Specifically, the danger is being in the path of the bullet once it leaves the muzzle, which means that to avoid the danger, you must get out of the line of fire. You can accomplish that by redirecting the line of fire or moving the target (body defense).

Any technique that moves your body by stepping, twisting or leaning requires more muscle activity and offers the gunman telltale signs, triggering his response to fire the weapon. Instead, your initial movement must be as undetectable and small as possible, and it must alter the line of fire. In most cases with krav maga, this redirection is made with a hand. Students train to use their hands without making any initial body movements—no leaning, no tensing up, no weight shifting. This makes the defensive technique more difficult for the attacker to detect. Only after the initial hand movement has begun should you initiate a body defense.

Krav maga teaches you to make initial redirections using only one hand. This results in smaller, less detectable movements, and it facilitates a body defense because the one-handed action turns your body slightly sideways. Two-handed defenses create bigger, easier-to-see motions, and they make a body defense impossible unless you drop down, which slows your ability to move in and finish the gunman. In addition, two-handed defenses decrease your length, while one-handed defenses allow you to stretch out, making the technique more effective at greater distances as well as at different angles.

You should redirect the gun off your body along the shortest path possible. In addition, you must redirect the line of fire in such a way that it travels across less vital areas. Krav maga's techniques move the weapon laterally, parallel to the ground along the shortest, straightest line possible. For example, if the weapon is pointed at the center of your chest, the redirection makes the line of fire travel from vital to nonvital areas whether you move it to the left or the right. This may seem like common sense, but many instructors of other arts prefer to push the gun upward, which means the line of fire travels from their chest to their throat to their mouth to their brain and then off their body.

THE ONE-HANDED GRAB

Krav maga instructors frequently teach a redirection and control technique with one hand. The two questions students most often ask are the following:

• Won't your hand get pinched or cut by the slide on a semi-automatic handgun?

• Won't the heat of the gun burn your hand when it fires?

The answer to both is "No." Not only will the slide not pinch you, but also the defense you use will most likely keep the slide from operating, thus preventing a new round from cycling into the chamber. On a revolver, the technique prevents the cylinder from turning and placing a new round in front of the hammer. And while a gun barrel will start to warm up after several rounds, it will not be uncomfortable.

—*J.W.*

GUN-ATTACK DEFENSE: The assailant (left) approaches from behind and places his weapon against the defender's back (1). The defender looks over his shoulder to ensure no weapon is in the assailant's other hand (2), then turns toward the attacker, making an arm and body motion to redirect the weapon without stepping (3). He immediately reaches out, anticipating the assailant's effort to draw the weapon back and reposition it to fire (4). He then bursts in, securing the gun hand at the wrist and delivering an elbow strike to the face (5). The defender takes away the weapon while maintaining eye contact, if possible (6), then retreats to safety.

CONTROL THE WEAPON

Once you've made the initial redirection, you must control the weapon. Remember that the gun-man will not be passive. The moment you defend yourself, he will fight to put the line of fire back on you, and he may even strike you to accomplish that. You must control the weapon so the line of fire can never be redirected at you. Even though krav maga techniques are effective at preventing more than one round (the one already chambered) from firing, you should always assume the weapon can continue to shoot.

Krav maga techniques assume that once you've made an initial redirection, the assailant will pull back on the weapon to put you in front of the muzzle again. (If he doesn't pull, the techniques are that much easier.) Therefore, you must burst in, putting your weight inward and downward on the gun. If the weapon remains up in a shooting position, he will have more control of it, but once you get the weapon down and in, his control will be limited. You must be prepared to move your feet to keep putting weight on the weapon even if he struggles or collapses from your punch.

COUNTERATTACK

No defense against a serious attack is complete unless it involves a counterattack, and whenever possible, you need to counterattack while you defend. In the case of a gun defense, you should counterattack as you take control of the weapon. If your strikes do not incapacitate the attacker, they will at least distract him so you can better control the gun.

Furthermore, a good counterattack will help you make a proper defense. For instance, when facing a threat from the front, krav maga's counterattack is a punch to the face. Properly executed, the blow not only inflicts damage but also helps you burst forward and put more weight on the gun.

When defending against a threat from behind, krav maga teaches you to deliver an elbow strike. Why an elbow instead of a punch? Because training to deliver an elbow (a short-range weapon) forces you to move in deep—a vital element when the gunman, in reaction to your initial defensive movement, will most likely pull the weapon toward himself and away from you. By training to burst in, you give yourself the best chance to trap the weapon.

DISARM

An effective technique must put you in a safe and effective position before to the disarm. On the street against an assailant putting up heavy resistance, you may not be able to take the weapon away, so the first measure of any gun defense must be, How safe does it keep you before the takeaway?

KRAV MAGA IN ACTION

In Lubbock, Texas, police officers responded to calls of an elderly woman in her own home posing a threat to those around her. Unable to contact the woman, the officers identified themselves and entered the home. The woman, unwilling to believe the officers were legitimate, armed herself with a handgun. As one of the officers rounded a corner, she put the gun to his head. The officer, who had recently gone through *krav maga* training, responded by redirecting the line of fire and controlling the weapon as he had been taught. He disarmed the woman without injury to himself or her.

—J.W.

By the same token, the disarm must keep you safe. Far too many instructors teach techniques that bring the line of fire right across the student's body. One "master" even has a video that shows a disarming technique that ends with the muzzle pointed at the student's face.

In addition, the technique must limit the danger potential for bystanders. For this reason, krav maga generally avoids sweeping leverage movements in which the gun follows a circular path from one side to the other. Done perfectly, these movements can be effective, but considering how much lower your performance will be under stress, such large-scale movements are likely to leave you and others in the line of fire.

Krav maga practitioners prefer short, explosive, snapping motions blended into a technique that breaks the attacker's hold on the gun without major (and possibly unpredictable) movements of his arms. The weapon is then removed from his grasp. Only when you are sure it is in your possession do you move off. If you think you have control of the weapon and begin to step away, the attacker could still have a partial grasp on it. As you retreat, you could place yourself back in the line of fire.

Your retreat is vital. Among the most common mistakes made in gun-defense training is taking the weapon but remaining in close proximity to the gunman. Once the weapon is yours, create distance between yourself and your attacker.

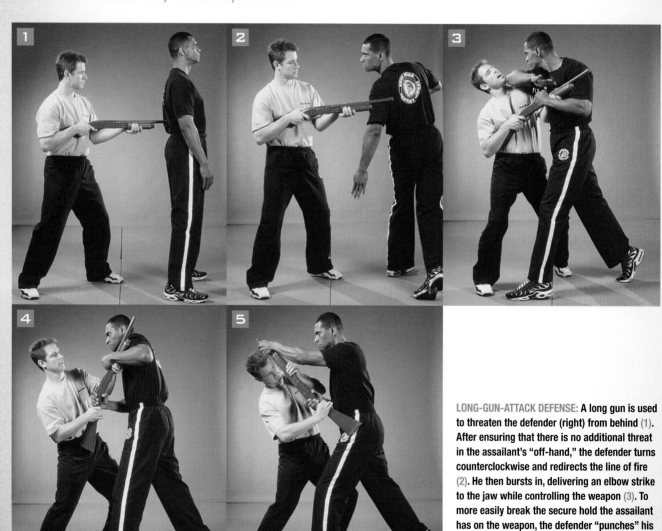

LONG-GUN-ATTACK DEFENSE: A long gun is used to threaten the defender (right) from behind (1). After ensuring that there is no additional threat in the assailant's "off-hand," the defender turns counterclockwise and redirects the line of fire (2). He then bursts in, delivering an elbow strike to the jaw while controlling the weapon (3). To more easily break the secure hold the assailant has on the weapon, the defender "punches" his shoulder upward (4). Sliding his left hand to the end of the barrel, the defender punches down at the assailant's head (5). He then takes away the gun and retreats.

USE OF THE GUN

Students often ask whether they are allowed to shoot the gunman once they have taken away his weapon. The answer depends on the context. This article cannot define and explain the legal ramifications of self-defense and the use of force in every part of the United States. Furthermore, such decisions must be made by you in the heat of the moment, not by a magazine article.

However, sound tactics must at least include the possibility of using the weapon if you believe your life is still in danger. If the gunman charges after you once you've taken his weapon, the assault clearly is not over. Consider his mental state in that situation: He threatened you with deadly force, you defended yourself and disarmed him, you are now armed, and he still attacks you. In this scenario, it makes tactical sense to retain the weapon and hold it in a position where it may be used. It will then be up to you to determine your own course of action.

A bigger issue is whether you are able to use the weapon. Consider the following: How do you clear a jammed weapon? What does "tap and rack" mean? Where is the safety on a Glock 30? Or a SIG Sauer P232? How do you hold and fire a cheap Tech-9? If you can't answer these questions, you probably shouldn't consider the object in your hand a firearm. Instead, think of it as a blunt object because you probably don't know how to operate it safely.

ULTIMATE KNIFE DEFENSE:
Haganah Survival Skills
for Beating the Blade

by Mike Lee Kanarek • *Black Belt December 2007*

THE WEAPON OF CHOICE in many violent crimes and rage attacks is the knife. The reason is simple: Knives are easily acquired by anyone who's planning to commit a crime because they're present in most homes, making them ideal weapons of opportunity. Furthermore, they're extremely efficient at inflicting injury, even in untrained hands. In many cases, the damage is fatal.

Knives are hard to detect and harder to avoid. When law-enforcement officers are asked what they fear most about violent struggles with criminals, they consistently say, "Him pulling out a knife." The apprehension is even greater among corrections officers, who face improvised blades wielded by inmates with nothing to lose.

The knife threat also pertains to civilians, who are more likely to be confronted by a blade than a bullet.

I had my own encounter with cold steel during my service in the Israeli Defense Force, and I can tell you that it's not like the movies would have you believe. I learned that whether you're a civilian, a law-enforcement officer or a soldier, things are never as clear and focused as they are at that moment. Your gut reaction is, Am I ready for this?

The goal of *haganah* is to enable you to answer in the affirmative.

COMPOSITION

Preparing to survive a knife attack is serious business and must include three phases of training. Phase one is learning to read the attack that your assailant is unleashing and identify the primary danger.

Phase two is developing the ability to choose and implement the right tactic to neutralize the danger.

Phase three is what Israelis call "stress training." It entails drills that desensitize your body and mind so they can handle the pressure despite overwhelming odds. This is the stage in which you make the abilities you developed in phase one and phase two instinctive and automatic. You build "muscle memory." Consider how human beings learn to walk: We don't think about it; we just do it. We're able to do that because we've developed muscle memory for the associated motions. And it occurred relatively quickly—within a few months, most likely. Haganah knife defense is learned the same way.

The third phase is the most important because it prepares you for reality. At the end of the day, it won't matter how many techniques you know. What matters is that you're trained in a way that keeps you from losing your composure under pressure—which is the only way you'll be able to deploy the right techniques.

LEARNING HOW TO READ

Before you can survive an edged-weapon attack, you must learn how to read the angle of the attack. Regardless of the assailant's objective—which may be to stab you, slash you or use a combination of the two—the knife must follow a trajectory from its starting point to your body. You must train your mind to identify the primary danger—the angle of attack—and that requires memorization. Once you can instantly recognize the angles, you'll be less likely to freeze up.

This stage of the engagement is crucial because you won't get a second chance to respond. If you mess up in a fistfight, you can absorb the punch or kick and come back. Not so in a knife fight.

It's also important to use footwork to "cut the angle on the attacker." That action moves you out of the knife's path. Often overlooked, footwork is the link between the mental skill of reading and the mechanics required to start your defense.

DOWNWARD SLASH: Mike Lee Kanarek (right) faces an armed attacker (1). When the slash begins, Kanarek angles away from the knife's trajectory and seizes the man's arm (2) before firing a kick into his groin (3). The *haganah* **expert capitalizes on the short-circuit effect of the kick and moves to a point of reference (4), after which he executes a knee thrust to the groin (5). Kanarek then takes him down while controlling his elbow to avoid being cut (6). He finishes with a strike to the carotid artery (7) and a disarm (8).**

DEFENSIVE PRINCIPLES

From the moment you cut the angle on your attacker, everything you do must be aggressive. Be decisive in your actions, neutralizing him as quickly as possible. Confidence plays a big role in this. Your mind-set must switch from victim to predator in the blink of an eye. And you need to harness your emotions to effectively manage your tactics. Easily said but not so easily done.

Confidence in performance comes from two sources. One, you must trust your defensive-tactics system. If the techniques you've learned have been tested on the battlefield, you'll trust yourself. Two, you must have undergone sufficient drilling to develop the aforementioned muscle memory. Those with poor muscle memory will pay a heavy price.

On a technical level, haganah knife defense follows a number of common principles. It doesn't rely on hundreds of techniques for all possible attacks. If you learn a separate technique for each

STRAIGHT STAB: Mike Lee Kanarek (left) is confronted by Ken Church (1). Kanarek moves off the thrust line and blocks the opponent's arm (2). Seizing the limb, Kanarek slams a right punch into Church's carotid artery (3). The blow short-circuits the enemy, enabling Kanarek to maneuver to a point of reference (4) and launch a knee strike to the groin (5). He then grabs the man's chin and twists for a neck break (6).

BLADE RECOMMENDATIONS

Martial artists need two types of training knives. First is a hard aluminum knife for practicing blocks. It simulates a real blade without subjecting you to the danger of being cut. You'll also need a sparring knife, preferably one that has a rubber blade that's forgiving so you don't injure your partner when you hit his hands during stress training—and vice versa.

In the end, though, the way you train is more important than what you train with. If you have a good training blade and an irresponsible teacher, you won't make much progress.

As far as a knife for everyday carry goes, your choice depends on your objective. If you're in the military, the fixed blade is king. As in training, the knife doesn't really matter because at the end of the day, every knife can cut and stab. What's important is how quickly you can deploy it. If you have a good knife with a fancy sheath and it takes you three seconds to remove it—and meanwhile the other guy has a kitchen knife that's already out—you'll be at a severe disadvantage.

At the civilian and law-enforcement level, the best choice is a folding knife. Choose a workhorse, one that will last a long time. Avoid delicate, high-tech blades. Before you buy, find out what type of steel is used. A V-30 blade will be very sharp but not serrated. It will cut like a scalpel, but it won't be effective once it's dented or dulled. I usually recommend a serrated blade because it more easily cuts through clothing. If you have a blade that's not serrated and you need to take out your opponent's mobility (cut the inside or outside tendon behind the knee) and he's wearing jeans that have gotten wet, you won't be slicing through. A serrated blade, however, will shred the fabric.

A good size for the blade of a folding knife is the width of your fist. It shouldn't be shorter or much longer. Half the blade's length is used for blocking, and the other half is for slashing and stabbing. If the blade is too short, you won't have enough to block with, and your opponent will slash through. If it's much longer, it won't fit in your pocket.

—MLK

angle of attack, the scanning process used by your brain, as well as your neuromuscular response, will be ineffective. You'll experience overload.

From the moment you cut the angle, the principle is simple: Seize the limb that's holding the knife to gain control of the weapon, then short-circuit the attacker, capture a point of reference and neutralize the threat. See the accompanying photos for details.

BATTLE-TESTED

When learning self-defense—and especially knife defense—you should use a proven method of engagement. Haganah techniques and strategies have survived the ultimate proving ground: the battlefields of the Middle East. That's why the Israeli combative systems have the advantage.

However, it's not just the system that's battle-tested; it's the training method. In the training used by the military and law enforcement, authorities have acknowledged that practicing simple tactics under stressful conditions constitutes the best method for enabling a person to defend himself on the street. That's why haganah incorporates specific stress drills to deal with knife defense. They're the final skill-enhancement tools needed to ensure that you'll walk away the survivor.

THROAT THREAT: The assailant presses his knife against Mike Lee Kanarek's throat (1). Kanarek places his hands alongside the man's forearm so he can deflect the blade while moving forward (2). Once he's bypassed the weapon and captured a point of reference (3), Kanarek effects an elbow strike to the carotid artery (4). While maintaining pressure on his neck, Kanarek aims a knee thrust at his thigh (5). To finish, he reaches behind the enemy's neck and grabs his chin (6), after which he takes him to the ground while controlling the arm so he can take away the knife (7).

OTHER SIDE OF THE COIN

In your quest for consummate knife-defense skill, you should also learn knife fighting. It's all about intelligence gathering. How can you protect against what you don't understand? Just as combat evolves, you must evolve from empty-hand-vs.-knife to knife-vs.-knife to maximize your ability.

It's in knife-vs.-knife training that you'll get a serious dose of reality and realize how slim your chance of fending off a skilled edged-weapon attacker really is. That's why I advise students to use equal or greater force whenever possible. If he has a knife, you'll want one, too. If you don't have one, look for an improvised weapon. Using your bare hands is your last resort. Because it's your last line of defense, the training must be especially rigorous.

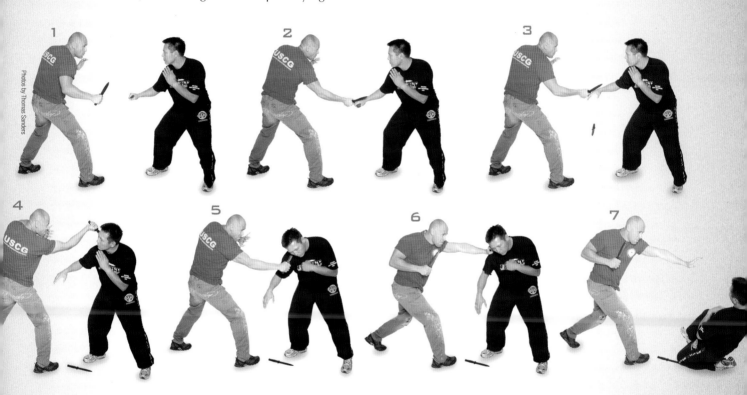

KNIFE SLASH: Mike Lee Kanarek (left) and Ken Church square off with training knives (1). Kanarek swiftly moves in and executes a slash to the hand (2). The cut causes the opponent to drop his weapon (3), and Kanarek capitalizes on the opening by stabbing him in the neck (4). The *haganah* instructor then changes the angle of the blade and slashes downward (5). He finishes by pushing the man away so he can continue his mission (6-7).

CONCLUSION

In any combat situation involving a knife, you'll probably get cut. To make sure you survive, you must select a training method with a track record. From the early days of the *Palmach* ("strike force") unit of the Haganah in the late 1940s and '50s to the days of the Israel Defense Force special ops to the present day in America, haganah has built a reputation as a combat-proven and battle-tested system. When you're facing a blade on the street, it may be all that stands between being a survivor and being a victim.

BLEEDING EDGE:
Martial Blade Concepts (MBC)
Represents the State of the Art in Knife Fighting
Part 1

by Michael Janich • Black Belt September 2009

KNIFE FIGHTING has always been one of the most misunderstood topics in self-defense. Although everyone agrees that the knife is a potent weapon, there's no consensus when it comes to effective edged-weapon tactics. Some practitioners swear by the traditional European and Asian systems. Others look to military combatives as the ultimate source of blade techniques. Still others regard prison-style knife tactics as the best.

So which methods should you bet your life on? That depends on what type of knife you carry and what situations you're likely to face. If you're a soldier carrying a full-size combat knife in a war zone, your needs and rules of engagement are different from those of a convict armed with a sharpened toothbrush or a civilian carrying a tactical folding knife.

My exploration of knife tactics began with the classic military systems. In addition to reading about and experimenting with the work of Anthony Drexel Biddle, William E. Fairbairn and John Styers, I had the rare privilege of consulting closely with the late Col. Rex Applegate and personally picking his brain on World War II-era knife combatives. I also thoroughly researched the works of early modern authorities like Michael D. Echanis, David E. Steele and James Keating, as well as masters of the Philippine and Indonesian systems. Every step of the way, I learned something—even if it was what not to do with a knife.

The result of my 30-plus years of training, research and analysis is Martial Blade Concepts. It draws heavily from battle-proven tactics taught in the Philippines and Indonesia and adapts those methods to the needs of modern personal defense. Although it can—and has—been adapted to military environments, it's primarily a self-defense system. As such, its greatest value lies in its relevance to the problem at hand: the effective defense of your life and the lives of loved ones against the types of attacks that occur in our society.

MBC is based on a number of fundamental concepts that define its reality-based self-defense focus and clearly separate it from knife systems that are unrealistic, poorly conceived or inappropriate for modern applications. Realistic defensive knife tactics are not about knife dueling. Knife fighting—at least the way I see it—is best defined as "learning how to fight effectively with a knife." As long as you're legally justified in bringing a knife into a defensive situation, it doesn't matter what type of weapon your attacker is armed with. Whether he's swinging a stick, a brick, a tire iron or a blade, your tactics must be sound and versatile enough to adapt to the situation. Don't limit yourself to training that focuses only on knife-vs.-knife dueling. Be able to apply your skills to the broadest possible set of defensive situations.

Accept that you'll fight with the knife you have when you're attacked. The design of the "ultimate fighting knife" will always be a hotly debated topic, but the truth is that the best fighting knife in the world is the one you have with you when the altercation starts, not the one back home in your sock drawer. Many of the designs recommended by self-proclaimed experts cannot be legally or practically carried by civilians on a daily basis. Understand that, accept it and choose your weapon accordingly.

Research the laws in your area and the areas you typically travel to and choose a knife that's legal in those jurisdictions. If possible, select one that has a training version that's mechanically identical to the live blade but allows you to safely make contact with your partner. Then tune your training to focus on the deployment and practical application of that weapon and make its carry part of your daily life.

It's essential to understand the cutting and puncturing performance of your carry knife so you know what it—and you—can do to a target. You need to have a clear understanding of its destructive

WOOD VS. STEEL: Against a longer weapon such as a stick, Michael Janich responds with a "meet"—cutting the attacker's flexor tendons (1-2) and staying on the inside to check the arm with his left hand (3). He follows up with a thrust to the armpit (4) and a cut through the biceps, nerve plexus and brachial artery as he leverages the weapon arm downward (5-6). Next, he does a backhand cut to the triceps (7), a check to the weapon-arm elbow (8) and a comma cut to the quadriceps (9-11) to end the encounter.

potential, and the only way to do that is to actually cut and puncture targets with it.

The best target for this phase of training is one that accurately simulates flesh-and-bone body parts and is covered with a layer of clothing. I use something I call a "pork man." I start with a 5-pound pork roast, then cut it lengthwise about halfway through its thickness and tie it around a 1-inch dowel with a generous amount of butcher twine (which replicates tendons and connective tissue). I wrap the entire thing in 20 to 30 layers of plastic wrap, tape down the ends and cover it with cloth—the leg of a pair of jeans, a sleeve from a jacket or something similar. The result is a good facsimile of the average man's forearm, upper arm or lower thigh—the preferred targets of MBC.

Obviously, before you attempt any live-blade cutting, you must have the requisite knife skills and take the proper safety precautions to avoid injury. It's best to train with an unsharpened knife for at least several months before attempting any cut.

Live-blade cutting allows you to validate the destructive capability of your carry knife against a realistic target and, in the process, gives you an accurate understanding of the resistance involved when cutting through clothing into flesh. During this part of testing, you should assess the effects of each cut and thrust. Be consistent with the techniques you use and make sure they're not contrived power swings.

Until you've invested the time to prove it to yourself, take my word for it: With proper skills, a sharp, high-quality folding knife with a 3-inch blade will cut "to the bone" on a pork man covered with medium-weight clothing.

Photos by Rick Hustead

AGAINST AN ANGLE NO. 1 ATTACK: As Matt Zavakos (right) attacks, Michael Janich evades and allows the arm to pass (1-2). Janich closes the gap and executes a backhand cut to the triceps (3). Driving forward, he checks and monitors the elbow and steps in deep with his left leg (4) to grind his Zavakos' knee into the ground (5). A cut to the Achilles tendon (6) and a stomp to the ankle (7-8) destroy the man's mobility and provide an opportunity for escape.

Real self-defense is all about "stopping power." In any fight, your goal is to get away safely—period. As such, the focus of your training should be to stop the attacker efficiently and decisively, to minimize injury to you and to create an opportunity for escape. Unfortunately, most knife systems confuse stopping power with killing power. If you defend yourself by delivering a lethal cut but that wound doesn't produce an immediate stopping effect, you're still in danger. Although your attacker may die, he has the opportunity to kill you before he does. That's not good enough.

Study human anatomy to learn what targets you can cut to reliably stop an attacker. Although most systems focus on closing the distance and delivering potentially lethal cuts and stabs to the torso or neck, the effects of those wounds aren't immediate, reliable or predictable.

Rather than going to martial arts sources, Internet forums or even military close-combat materials—such as the widely touted but wildly inaccurate Fairbairn Timetable of Death—I researched stopping power based on an analysis of knife attacks and interviews with trauma doctors, paramedics, physical therapists and medical professionals who regularly see the results of knife wounds. After hearing about many examples of people who were stabbed repeatedly in the torso but didn't stop fighting, it became clear that there had to be a better way.

A foundational element of the Philippine martial arts is "defanging the snake," or biomechanical cutting. Basic anatomy teaches that muscles pull on tendons to move bones. If a tendon is severed or the muscle powering the action is cut deeply enough, the structure that enables movement is immediately compromised. Traditional defanging with a knife involves cutting the flexor tendons or the muscles on the inside of the forearm to take away an attacker's ability to grip a weapon. MBC expands on this by focusing on three specific target priorities:

1. the forearm and flexor tendons to destroy the grip
2. the biceps and triceps to destroy coordinated motion of the weapon arm
3. the quadriceps above the knee to destroy mobility

Such cuts not only target the tendons and muscles, thus producing an immediate disabling result, but also can be used to attack adjacent nerves and major arteries, providing an immediate secondary method of disabling the limb and achieving delayed stopping power through blood loss.

This approach has been reviewed by trauma surgeons, neurologists and physical therapists, including the staff of the International School of Tactical Medicine. All have found it to be medically sound and agree that, applied properly, it will produce predictable disabling effects.

That's why I recommend basing your tactics on natural, easily learned movements that take into account human instinct and the physiological effects of life-threatening stress. The natural reactions you must allow for include the "startle response" and a degradation of fine- and complex-motor skills. Although it's possible to train to mitigate instinctive reactions to stress so you can apply complicated tactics, it takes lots of time and intense training. A smarter approach is to accept that you'll respond instinctively and build your tactics on the foundation of that instinct.

In training, focus on patterns of motion that emphasize simplicity and commonality of technique. Rather than learning specific responses for each attack, learn a small number of versatile moves that can be reflexively applied to a range of situations. MBC uses a system of angles like the Philippine arts do, but the angles are based on your point of view and used primarily to identify and categorize incoming attacks. Together, those strategies yield a system that promotes rapid, reflexive decision-making followed by the application of instinctive and effective techniques.

It's essential to develop your abilities using methods that involve the repetition of critical skills in challenging conditions. Repetition is the mother of all skill. Repetition under realistic stress is the mother of truly reliable skill. The "flow" drills taught in the Philippine arts can provide challenging and time-efficient training methods. In their rote form, they isolate and refine specific skills. At higher

Photos by Rick Hustead

TARGETING PRIORITIES AND STOPPING POWER: The opponent attacks with a high right forehand cut (1), and Michael Janich defends with a "pass"—leaning backward and cutting the flexor tendons of the forearm (2). After the arm moves to the inside (3), Janich follows up with a backhand cut to the triceps (4) and closes the distance to check the man's elbow (5) and off-balance him (6). Janich finishes with a comma cut—a thrust-and-cut combination to the quadriceps (7-8). Note how he "walks through" the technique for maximum power and to begin his escape (9).

levels of training, you'll find yourself performing individual drills more quickly and with greater intensity, and you'll spontaneously transition from one drill to another without cueing your partner. This training format promotes quick actions and closely replicates the level of adrenal stress you'll experience in a real attack.

Integrating drill practice into a dynamic "chess game" also allows you to experience what it's like to react to various attack angles from many initial hand positions. In doing so, you program yourself to choose the most structurally efficient responses to attacks and overcome your opponent's checks, grabs and counters.

BLEEDING EDGE
Counter-Blade Concepts
Part 2

by Michael Janich • October 2009

DEFENDING YOURSELF empty handed against a knife attack is one of the most terrifying scenarios imaginable. In such a dire situation, there are no surefire techniques that will guarantee that you'll emerge unscathed. However, there are techniques and systems that can significantly increase your chances of surviving.

My interest in edged-weapon tactics began more than 30 years ago when I embarked on a quest to learn empty-hand defenses against knife attacks. The art I was studying didn't teach knife fighting, so our defenses weren't geared toward dealing with realistic attacks. When my training partners and I turned up the heat and attacked with intent, the contrived defenses invariably fell apart.

I later learned that the best place to look for weapon defenses is within the martial cultures that specialize in the use of that particular weapon. Because the Philippine and Indonesian arts include some of the most effective small-knife techniques ever developed, they provide a great foundation for knife defense—which is why they served as the basis for much of my study.

Unfortunately, anytime a system is developed within an isolated culture, it tends to reflect its own methods. In other words, it focuses on defending against its own specific attacks rather than "street" attacks. It also reflects the legal and cultural norms of that society. Both shortcomings make these systems somewhat less suitable for modern self-defense.

Counter-Blade Concepts (CBC) is a system of empty-hand tactics I devised for use against edged weapons. It draws from the proven tactics of the Philippine and Indonesian arts yet is consistent with the training needs and legalities of Western culture. In developing CBC, my first goal was to understand how knife attacks actually happen. I did that by collecting and analyzing film and video footage from all over the world. By identifying the common elements, I was able to define the problem.

Based on that understanding, I began to extract and modify traditional counter-knife tactics to get them to work against real attacks. My partners and I tested them with increasing speed and intensity. I then introduced them to students at seminars to see whether they could learn them easily within a reasonable time. So far, the results have been outstanding.

One of the key components of CBC is its "anatomy of a knife attack." Based on my analysis, assaults usually unfold in one of many way.

1. They start at close range.
2. Typically, the weapon isn't brandished beforehand.
3. Most people are right-handed, so most attacks are right-handed.
4. Attackers typically use gross-motor skills with forehand motions.
5. The nonweapon hand is used to grab and gauge distance.
6. Attacks involve repetitive motions; they're seldom a single cut or thrust.

With these points in mind, I based CBC on a sequence of actions that form the foundation of its self-defense tactics.

1. Minimize injury to yourself.

2. Counter and disable immediately, or draw your own weapon, if possible.

3. If you cannot disable immediately, maintain contact and control the attacking limb.

4. Attack and disable.

5. If you're duty bound (a police officer, security guard etc.), restrain, control and disarm.

6. If you're not duty bound, break contact, evaluate, scan and escape.

PRACTICAL EMPTY-HAND COMBATIVES: DAMITHURT SILAT

Facing a knife is bad enough, but it gets worse: Research has shown that most aggressors don't brandish their blades before attacking. As such, you won't know it's a knife attack until you're already bleeding. If your approach to self-defense uses different responses for armed and unarmed attacks, you may be setting yourself up for failure.

For me, the solution has been the following: Strive to master one skill set that offers as much common ground as possible. Whether you're fighting with a knife, a stick, an improvised weapon or your bare hands, you shouldn't have to change your body mechanics, footwork, low-line kicks and overall patterns of movement. That way, you have less to learn, and no matter what weapon or weapons you might have at your disposal, you can use them effectively.

When it comes to unarmed tactics, you should assume that your attacker has a weapon. If his "punch" happens to have a sharp piece of steel at the end of it, at least you know that your defenses are sound.

The core of your skill set should be your empty-hand system; in my case, it's based on various Philippine and Indonesian systems, military combatives and the Japanese arts. Like Counter-Blade Concepts, it's designed to first limit damage to you, then control the attacking limb, create a power base and use gross-motor-skill strikes to destroy your opponent's mobility so you can escape. To make things easier, you can focus on using your strong side; there's no need to force yourself to be ambidextrous.

For years, the aforementioned system had no name. My students kept pestering me to call it something, so I thought about it long and hard. One day, while applying a particularly painful technique in training, a student exclaimed, "Damn, that hurts a lot!" And that was the answer.

In honor of the Indonesian *silat* systems I liked so much, I called it "damithurt silat." My stick-fighting system honors the Philippine arts with the name "sobadiwan eskrima." When you say them together, you get "Damn, it hurts a lot—so bad I wanna scream." Like the tactics they represent, the names of the systems are simple, effective and easy to remember.

—M.J.

Once you understand this sequence, you must grasp the significance of the term "concepts" in the CBC name. The use of that word doesn't mean the skills that make up the system cannot be quantified; it was chosen to emphasize the fact that principles are more important than techniques. The principles are expressed in the four phases of training: Deflect and Counter, Control and Counter, Returning Blade, and Combined Skills.

PHASE 1

The best counter-knife techniques are based on the same body mechanics as the best knife-fighting methods. The only difference is that instead of using your bladed weapon to disable the attacker, you use your natural weapons and any improvised weapons that are available. Defensively, however, very little changes.

Consequently, the first phase is Deflect and Counter. It focuses on blocking and redirecting incoming attacks with the back of the forearm and checking with the palm. No attempt is made to capture the attacker's limb or disarm him. Instead, you use a checking or passing action to interrupt his motion and create an opening for a finger strike to the eyes. Attacking the eyes disrupts his vision, causes pain and often makes him reflexively drop his weapon.

You can follow up with low-line kicks to the ankle or knee to create a "mobility kill" that leaves your opponent unable to pursue you as you escape. That also buys you time to deploy your weapon, if you have one.

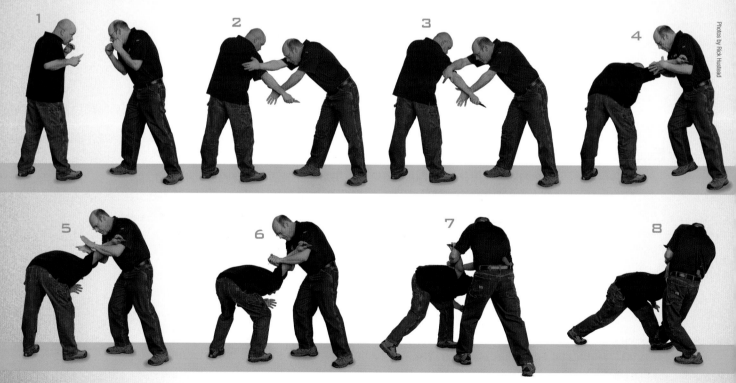

Photos by Rick Hustead

EMPTY HAND VS. KNIFE: Against a low-line thrust, Michael Janich (right) "hollows out" and stops the knife arm with a split-X block (1-2). He hooks the arm above the elbow to prevent a second thrust (3) and pulls it to his chest while rotating the limb to lock the elbow (4). Janich "saws" on the triceps tendon (5) and secures the arm with a palm-into-palm grip (6). He then steps back with his right foot, causing the attacker to step forward (7) and expose his left leg to an ankle-breaking stomp kick (8).

Deflect and Counter is a hit-and-run approach to empty-hand knife defense and the primary tactic in a reality-based knife program. It doesn't require any grappling or controlling actions and is designed to immediately debilitate your attacker so you can escape.

PHASE 2

The tactics of Control and Counter are used when you can't hit and run to create distance. If you're in a confined space or you're a law-enforcement officer who must subdue an armed attacker, the goal is to control the knife limb securely while you deliver blows and/or throws to incapacitate him.

FLASHLIGHT VS. KNIFE: The CBC system also incorporates improvised weapons as a means to defend against a knife. Here, the assailant (left) initiates a reverse-grip stab to the neck (1-2). Michael Janich, armed with a tactical flashlight, uses the Philippine *hubud* tactic to deflect the attack with his left hand (3) and then his right forearm (4). He checks the arm downward and shines the light into the man's eyes (5). Taking advantage of the momentary blindness, Janich uses his left hand to drive the opponent's head back (6) while he steps through to deliver a strike to the face (7).

The best way to learn this phase is via the Seven-Position CBC Flow Drill. It teaches defenses for the four primary zones (angles No. 1 through No. 4, or high left, high right, low left and low right), two defenses for thrusts to the lower abdomen (low angle No. 5) and a defense for a thrust to the upper chest, neck or face (high angle No. 5).

The aim of the drill is to teach you how to control the attacker's arm in such a way that you limit his mobility to one joint: the shoulder. Rather than focusing on "stripping" the knife or disarming the wielder, you bypass the hand and wrist to control the entire arm. As such, the approach works against all edged weapons, including box cutters and razors that cannot be stripped by traditional methods. The conceptual basis also makes the moves effective against other ballistic weapon attacks, as well as static, mugging-style attacks effected with knives or handguns.

Each control position can be used as a takedown that's followed by restraint-and-control tactics (i.e., handcuffing). For civilians, the positions are primarily used to create a power base that enables the delivery of disabling strikes—hand techniques, low-line kicks and arm breaks. The control positions can also be used in conjunction with throws that not only destroy an attacker's mobility by taking him off his feet but also exploit the largest and handiest impact weapon you have: the ground. Even better, all of them are compatible with improvised weapons.

PHASE 3

The Returning Blade phase is exactly what it sounds like—feeding the attacker's blade back at him. Although it can be done by disarming him and using his weapon against him, you should avoid that for two reasons.

From a legal standpoint, if you're unarmed and your attacker has a knife, disarming him and then using his knife against him may be viewed as excessive force. If you end up in court, you'll have to prove that you acted in self-defense. Your initial response is easily justified; however, once you took

STICK VS. KNIFE: To show how the tactics of Martial Blade Concepts apply to the stick, Michael Janich (right) faces Matt Zavakos (1). Zavakos opens with a high forehand cut, which causes Janich to fade back and strike his wrist (2). Janich follows through (3) with a backhand strike to the elbow (4-5), a check to immobilize the arm (6) and a full-power blow to the shin to break the leg and destroy the man's mobility (7-8). The motions are identical to the MBC knife-based technique but are adapted to use the stick to hit bones.

EMPTY HAND VS. KNIFE: Counter-Blade Concepts is designed to integrate seamlessly with the use of other weapons. In this application of the same split-X defense, Michael Janich (right) blocks the initial thrust (1-2) and controls the elbow like before (3). However, he opts to pass the attacker's arm to his right (4). He then uses his left arm to push the knife arm away as he pivots to his right and begins to draw his handgun (5). Moving behind him, he's in position to fire into the man's pelvis if he continues his attack (6). The downward angle minimizes the chance that the bullet will hit a bystander should Janich miss his target.

possession of the knife and used it on an unarmed person—even one who was trying to kill you moments before—you'll be viewed as a criminal.

From a practical standpoint, disarming an assailant is difficult and dangerous, especially when his knife is a box cutter that can do significant damage to you but offers little leverage. It's safer and easier to turn his knife back on him while he's holding it.

Technically, you must keep yourself safe while you obtain some control of his limb. You then use your hands to effect a counterforce motion (i.e., push-pull) against his arm to collapse it at the elbow and direct his hand back toward him. Combine that action with body positioning, the use of anatomical struts and levers, and low-line trapping and destruction, and you'll make the return of his blade rather uncomfortable for him. Remember that your goal is still to disable him and escape.

PHASE 4

There's no foolproof counter-knife technique—which is why CBC focuses on concepts. It's also why the final phase of CBC emphasizes integrating the first three phases to create a system of back-ups. You flow from one tactic to another based on your opponent's energy and intent, as well as his effectiveness. Outcome is always emphasized over technique, and improvisation is encouraged.

The Combined Skills phase focuses on reference points, or specific physical relationships between you and your attacker. By understanding those structures and learning how to immediately recognize them in a dynamic situation, you can transition from one tactic to another spontaneously and reflexively while maintaining your safety.

Defending yourself against an edged weapon while empty handed is always going to be a worst-case scenario. I developed CBC to provide a practical, logical and effective system of tactics that will increase your survivability in such situations and dovetail seamlessly with weapon-based tactics. I continue to research, refine and validate it because that's the only way to ensure that a reality-based system remains state of the art.

THOU SHALT NOT KILL?
The Truth Behind the Use of Deadly Force in Self-Defense

by Frank Gannon • Black Belt June 2010

IN *SPIDER-MAN,* Uncle Ben told Peter Parker, "With great power comes great responsibility." The fact that the statement originates from a comic-book character doesn't make it any less true. It's especially applicable to the martial arts and the use of deadly force. Deadly force is the most serious issue you can confront. The martial arts are based on the premise that force may be necessary to protect human life, which is why so many techniques empower even an unarmed person to kill an attacker easily. Civilized society, out of necessity, enacted rules to govern such conduct, and it's in your best interest to understand them before you use them.

Many rumors, misconceptions and falsehoods get tossed about by martial artists while discussing deadly force and self-defense. On this issue, engaging in guesswork is dangerous, for the improper use of deadly force can result in the double tragedy of the imprisonment of one party and the death of another. The purpose of this article is to provide a basic framework for understanding the way that the law views deadly force in the context of self-defense.

RULES AND REGULATIONS

Much of the confusion that surrounds the law of self-defense stems from the fact that it differs from state to state and country to country. Although the statutes have much in common, they can vary significantly. For simplicity, this article will address the views held by the majority of states. There's no guarantee that your state follows all, or any, of the rules that will be discussed—which is why you should review your local laws before taking action. The easiest way to read the statutes that apply to you is to visit the Web site of your state legislature.

DEFINITIONS AND SITUATIONS

"Deadly force" refers to force that's intended, or known by the person using it, to be capable of causing death or serious bodily injury. "Nondeadly force" is the term for all other types of force.

While nondeadly force is permitted in many self-defense scenarios, deadly force is justified only in the most extreme circumstances. Before resorting to any level of force, even nondeadly force, certain circumstances must first exist. In general, you must have the reasonable belief that force is immediately necessary to prevent the other person from unlawfully causing you physical harm. If someone hurls insults at you but shows no signs of physical aggression, there is no legal justification for using physical force against him.

You must have a reasonable belief that the other person's conduct is unlawful. If a police officer is performing a lawful arrest on you, you typically have no right to self-defense. In general, you're not allowed to use force to resist an arrest by a peace officer, even if the arrest is unlawful. However, some states—including Texas, Tennessee and Arizona—permit the use of force in self-defense if the officer uses more force than is necessary to make the arrest.

BUYER BEWARE

This article is not intended to be a comprehensive statement of the law or legal opinion. It merely presents a general overview and framework of the law at the time of its writing. Remember that laws differ from one state to another, and they change over time. Cases are overturned, statutes are repealed and new laws are laid down. The information provided here should not be relied on as a defense in any criminal or civil legal proceedings. If you find yourself in legal trouble or have a serious legal question, contact an attorney.

—F.G.

You must have a reasonable belief that the other person poses an immediate physical threat. If he's shouting threats at you but shows no immediate intent to act on them, you're not justified in using force. On the other hand, most states hold that if he raises a clenched fist as if to strike you or lunges violently toward you, his actions represent an immediate physical threat.

You must reasonably believe that immediate action is necessary to defend yourself against the threat. If a person threatens to take violent actions at some point in the future but shows no signs of immediate violence, there's no justification for using force.

The amount of force used must be reasonable given your understanding of the circumstances at the time it's used. If the aggressor shoves you while you're in line at the ballpark, you're not justified in breaking his arm.

The right to use force in self-defense lasts only as long as the threat lasts. If a person begins making threats of immediate violence toward you but calms down and shows no further signs of violence, you have no justification to use force.

Force may not be used in response to verbal provocations alone. If a man in a bar asks you to step outside to resolve a dispute, you can't punch him in the face.

You're generally not justified in using force against another when you're the one who did the provoking.

You cannot dare someone to hit you and then claim it as justification for self-defense.

If an attacker abandons the confrontation or clearly communicates an intent to do so, your right to use force against him stops. If someone sucker-punches you and then flees the scene, you can't track him down and pummel him. However, the right to use force stops only when the conflict has ended. The attacker must have clearly abandoned the confrontation. If he makes a "strategic retreat" to gain a more advantageous position to continue his assault, he hasn't abandoned the confrontation, and you retain the right to use force to protect yourself.

DEADLY FORCE

Generally speaking, deadly force is justified in situations in which you're justified in using non-deadly force against another person in self-defense and you reasonably believe that it's immediately necessary to prevent him from causing you death or serious bodily injury.

Most states hold that you're justified in using it to protect a third person if, under the circumstances as you reasonably believe them to be, you would have been legally justified in using deadly force if you were that third person and you reasonably believe that intervention is immediately necessary to protect him or her. For example, if you believe you're witnessing a murder, most states hold that you're justified in using deadly force against the attacker.

The use of deadly force in the protection of property is prohibited in most states. However, it can be justified in some circumstances when the theft of property is involved. For example, if an armed robber threatens you with immediate death or serious bodily injury, the use of deadly force is justified. On the other hand, in a close call with a pickpocket who places you in no reasonable fear of serious bodily injury or death, deadly force isn't permitted.

Some states, such as Nebraska and Texas, allow the use of deadly force to protect property from the immediate commission of certain crimes such as burglary or robbery. However, even in such situations, it's justified only if the use of nondeadly force would expose you or others to a substantial risk of death or injury.

DUTY TO RETREAT

Many states have ruled that a person may use deadly force only in situations in which there's no opportunity to retreat beforehand. Alaska, Connecticut, Delaware, Hawaii, Massachusetts, Maine, North Dakota, Nebraska, New Hampshire, New Jersey, New York and Pennsylvania are among them. This duty typically doesn't require retreat within your residence when you've been threatened with death or serious bodily injury.

In states that don't have an explicit statutory duty to retreat, important issues may still arise concerning the opportunity to retreat. This question often involves the factors that are considered in determining the reasonableness of the belief that deadly force was immediately necessary. If you could have easily fled the scene of the attack rather than resorting to deadly force, it becomes highly questionable whether such force was immediately necessary.

COMMON SENSE

The most potent tool in your arsenal is common sense. An oft-quoted maxim in martial arts schools is, The best block of all is to not be there. The same wisdom holds true in the legal arena. The legal justifications discussed in this article come into play only after an altercation has begun. By avoiding risky situations, you minimize the likelihood that violent force will be necessary. If nothing happens, no explanation—and no defense attorney—will be needed.

Other products from Black Belt Books

BRUCE LEE'S FIGHTING METHOD:
The Complete Edition

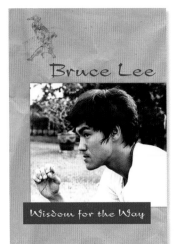

BRUCE LEE:
Wisdom for the Way

TAO OF JEET KUNE DO

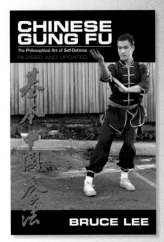

CHINESE GUNG FU:
The Philosophical Art
of Self-Defense
(Revised and Updated)

**THE ULTIMATE GUIDE TO
JEET KUNE DO**

CHINATOWN JEET KUNE DO:
Essential Elements of Bruce
Lee's Martial Art

**THE ULTIMATE GUIDE TO
KNIFE COMBAT**

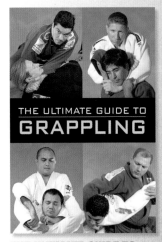

**THE ULTIMATE GUIDE TO
GRAPPLING**

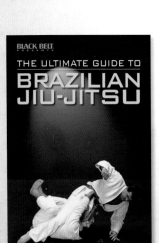

**THE ULTIMATE GUIDE TO
BRAZILIAN JIU-JITSU**

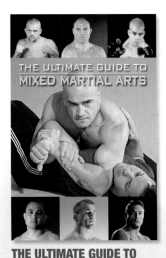

**THE ULTIMATE GUIDE TO
MIXED MARTIAL ARTS**

To subscribe
to the world's
No. 1 martial art's
magazine, call toll-free:
(800) 266-4066

To order, call toll-free: (800) 581-5222 or visit www.blackbeltmag.com/shop